LinkedIn Marketing

Step by Step on LinkedIn Marketing. How to Promote and Sell Anything through LinkedIn

Contents

Introduction

LinkedIn is a word that gets thrown around quite a bit. You may hear it from a classmate or in discussion with your colleagues. Despite how frequently it may come up, it is possible you still don't know everything about LinkedIn. So, what is LinkedIn?

LinkedIn is a social platform whose design makes it suitable for use by professionals. Unlike Facebook that has more focus on your personal life, LinkedIn is a social platform for your career life. It is crucial you learn as much as you can about this platform if you want to enjoy the massive benefits it has to offer.

An Introduction to the LinkedIn Platform

It doesn't matter your position; you can be a freshman at a college in search of a job, a local business owner, or a marketing executive at a top company in the country, you will surely find the LinkedIn platform very useful. As long as you are serious about moving your career to the next level and opening up opportunities for growth, you can benefit from the connections to other professionals that LinkedIn offers.

Looking at the dynamics of LinkedIn, you can liken it to attending a networking event. These events provide an opportunity for you to physically interact with other professionals in your industry, exchange business cards, and learn about one another. This is what happens on LinkedIn, and the only difference is that the event is virtual.

Like followers on Twitter and friends on Facebook, LinkedIn offers these features in the form of "connections." A connection is a user that you add to your network to support the growth of this network. Using the contact information of your connection or through a private message, it is possible to start a conversation with your connections.

1

Your profile on LinkedIn displays your experience and achievements as a professional so you can attract like-minded individuals.

In terms of general features and layout, there are several similarities between LinkedIn and Facebook. The features are easy to navigate if you have a basic knowledge of the Facebook platform with the significant difference being the focus on professionals.

To ensure you become an expert in the use of LinkedIn to achieve progress in your career, you will find a lot of information in the chapters that follow. These include what LinkedIn is all about, setting up a profile and company page, the importance of LinkedIn to your brand, and more. You will also find information on how to increase your number of connections, set up ads and many more.

Chapter 1

LinkedIn Basics

Generally, the evolution of social media has opened new frontiers of advertising and business promotion to professionals. Most business owners and professionals now have some basic understanding of how Facebook, Twitter, LinkedIn, Instagram, and a host of other social media platforms work. However, LinkedIn is one social platform that has mainly not been used to its optimal level.

Interestingly, it is the perfect platform suitable for B2B marketers. It has operated for years as a platform not only to promote business but also for job owners and professionals to connect with each other. Due to its impact, the financial value placed on LinkedIn by Microsoft, its acquirer, stands at a record $26billion ("LinkedIn Claims Half a Billion Users", 2017).

But while LinkedIn has been in use for years, it has not been optimally used by potential users. The newcomers on this platform only end up creating a profile that they do not derive more significant benefits from. This is partly due to the complexity of the platform and the intimidating intricacies in the process of using LinkedIn.

Regardless of the several complaints by would-be LinkedIn users, the platform remains one of the most formidable content marketing and social media networking opportunities for professional individuals, businesses, and business owners. This is the best time to start using LinkedIn if you've not started or hitherto aren't active on it.

In this chapter, we will look at some of the ample opportunities this social media network offers you to navigate the fantastic social world of business. But first, let's delve deeper into what LinkedIn is all about.

What is LinkedIn?

Regarded as the world's leading online site for networking with professionals, LinkedIn is home to close to 600 million users. Specifically, a 2018 study showed that the number of LinkedIn subscribers stood at over 590 million users, and the number continues to increase steadily (Cooper, 2019). As a global network, LinkedIn has users spanning more than 200 countries of the world. LinkedIn users cut across various professions, jobs, businesses, and industries. It is merely a network to give and tap into expertise, talents, and skills in multiple industries.

LinkedIn has indeed revolutionized how social media marketing and networking operate with its vast reach and search functionality. So, whether you're looking for a job, seeking better offers, exploring new industries and areas, expanding your social network, increasing your visibility, developing your personal skill or brand, or enhancing your professional prospects, then LinkedIn is for you. It's easy to set up a profile on the platform, connect with friends, and maintain networking connections. LinkedIn opens you to channels to look for employment; to find business opportunities; recruit and employ competent recruits and talents, and to stay connected with professional contacts; to engage connects who embrace new career and change career roles.

Unlike other popular social media platforms ranging from Instagram, Facebook, and Twitter that have professional and business functions as after-thought, LinkedIn was originally built with these functions in mind. This social network is specifically designed for the purpose of helping with job-seekers, professionals, businesses, business owners, and industry persons. It is targeted at harnessing the benefits of professional networking online. It is remarkably effective for building connections and generating ideas and leads for businesses, entrepreneurs, and professionals willing to bolster their brand.

How Does LinkedIn Function for Networking?

LinkedIn allows users to connect with people that they know. It could be people in their phone contact list or email list. In other words, LinkedIn enables you to connect with individuals you know and those who are linked up via others. You could also connect with the people in your LinkedIn connections. With the network serving as a virtual mixer, you can create a relationship with industry experts, and business success stories. Try to build a standard profile. Upload a clean, clear picture of your face and include a catchy but accurate summary of yourself. Never leave out important facts about yourself, your career, your work experience, skills, educational history, etc. Be active; pay attention to people in your industry. Comment and like posts of important people in the industry; join a forum that will enhance your connection growth and expansion. Bear in mind that your activity brings about your connection growth.

What is LinkedIn Used for?

It is important to reiterate that LinkedIn is more than a social media network. It is a platform for professionals and business people who want to grow in their career. In that light, there are a few things people use this platform for.

To Grow Your Network

Whether you are a seasoned networker or a novice, you have a terrain to flourish in LinkedIn. You can maintain and capitalize on many professional networks on the platform. Networking on LinkedIn can be more efficient without losing the chance to make connections via face-to-face interactions.

Join or Create a Group

LinkedIn offers various professional networks, groups, and communities you can join and link up with. LinkedIn networks could be your alma mater, experts in specific area and industry, philanthropy, people with shared vision and interest, football club, etc. You can also link up with people you desire to meet but are not in your network.

To Create Opportunities

LinkedIn offers one of the biggest networks that create opportunities for gainful employment and business growth. These opportunities are ample on the network, and you can tap into it. It helps expedite a job search and create new opportunities for businesses.

Business Ventures

LinkedIn is for you if you're an established or emerging entrepreneur, allowing you to delve into the high-end economy. LinkedIn offers a range of options that help you promote your business and the services you render. You can purchase targeted ads and publish strategic content. The network also offers tools that aid you in tracking your engagement and reach.

Status Updates

To build an enviable LinkedIn profile, you will also need to post regularly and update your status with informative and relevant updates. You can post a well-written article on areas and things you're passionate about. Curate content relating to areas of your interest. The more you're involved, the more you are likely to get noticed and find connections.

Blog

With LinkedIn, you have access to sharing and reading articles that you write. This blogging feature gives you leverage to showcase thought leadership. It is also a great feature to leverage on if you're looking at changing careers and moving to a new industry or transitioning to new areas of interest, passion, and commitment.

To Build a Platform

LinkedIn allows you to make sense of passion. So, if there is an interest you're passionate about or a message you want to share, LinkedIn offers the tools to achieve that. You can become an influencer and have a lot of connections and followers.

To Locate Your Tribe

Your tribe is not necessarily your ethnic group. It is those who share business interests and ideas with you. Linking up with them is a fantastic means to grow your network, expand your professional community and interface with people in the industry who matter

Comment on posts

Being an active LinkedIn user does not mean acquiring new followers and joining new Groups and communities. Besides, you have to make comments to posts from industry experts. Seek advice; ask relevant questions relating to your career, skills, and industry. You can create and post hypothetical stories that will ask questions to elicit information. The more active you are by posting and commenting, the more you're able to make more meaningful connections that will help your career objectives

Job Search

Never underestimate or doubt the tons of opportunities offered through LinkedIn. The network opens your personal brand, links you up with prospective employers, allowing you to create an 'intimidating' profile and a visible online resume that highlights your skills, credentials, and work experience. It will enable you to get recommendations and endorsements from colleagues and connections. In a more comprehensive level, LinkedIn gives you the capacity to run in-depth job searches with the help of keywords, and capitalizing on endorsements and recommendations from those you are connected to.

For Following the Leaders

LinkedIn helps trendsetters, companies, and industry leaders to share their updates, messages, and influence individuals who aspire to grow.

Search Profiles

LinkedIn offers tools for you to meet a targeted audience and opportunities. You can connect with other professionals outside the random networking events. You have the chance to search for and review other's profile. You're able to access people's profile, thereby opening you up to their education and work history, skills, interests, and successes.

Companies

Myriads of companies and brands make use of LinkedIn, and you find them with daily update of profiles from the industry in which they operate. They regularly have updates about company news, leadership changes, market research, and lots more. These updates provide the kind of information job seekers and competitive analysts need to be able to grow.

Individuals

LinkedIn serves as a platform where individuals who want to excel in their career boost their presence. LinkedIn tags these visionary potential successes with the sought-after "Influencer" badge on their profiles. LinkedIn allows these individuals who have attained the status of an influencer the opportunity to frequently share their blog posts, status updates, and videos. In fact, as a user of LinkedIn, you can follow these high-level individuals whose thought leadership and ideas can transform and enhance your life and career.

Features offered by LinkedIn

Below are a few of the fundamental features offered to you by LinkedIn. They include:

- Home: The instant you are logged in on the platform, your home feed shows you the posts recently made by your connections, professionals, and the pages of companies you are following. It is also called the news feed.

- Profile: This displays your name, location, picture, what you do, among others at the top. Underneath this, you have the capacity to modify various sections like your work experience, education, and a host of others just like you would write on a typical CV or resume.

- Jobs: LinkedIn shows you various kinds of job listings posted each day by employers. Also, LinkedIn will endorse specific jobs to you using your present information. This will include where you are located and your optional job presence which you have the capacity to fill, so you get job listings tailored to you.

- My Network: This is where you will find all the people you are presently connected with on the platform. If you place your mouse over this option, you can see a range of other options which will let you find others you know and include contact. You can also find your alumni this way.

- Search Bar: You are privy to a very reliable search feature which LinkedIn offers that lets you screen your results using various fields. Hit the "Advanced" option next to the search bar to locate specific jobs, companies, professionals, and a host of others.

- Messages: To begin a conversation with another individual you are connected with, you can use this feature. With this, you can send them a message privately via LinkedIn, and you can also include photos, attachments, etc.

- Interests: Aside from the professionals you follow, LinkedIn also allows you to follow a specific interest. These range from groups to company pages based on interest or location.

- Notifications: Similar to other social media platforms, LinkedIn comes with a notification feature which informs you when someone invites you to join something, endorses you, or requests you look through a post you may have an interest in.

- Pending Invitations: When you are invited by other professionals to connect with them, you get a notification which you need to approve. After approval, you become connected with the person and show up on each other's networks.

When you sign-up for the LinkedIn basic account, these are the core features you will observe instantly. There are more features the platform offers, many of which you can get access to if you upgrade to a premium account. We will be covering more of this later in this book.

Features That Can Be Beneficial to Your Business

As opposed to the basic features, the platform also offers some other features that can be beneficial to your business, which can also help in enhancing your professional status.

- LinkedIn Learning: If you need answers to questions, or perhaps you love learning or need more information regarding a specific topic, this is where to go. It offers you the capacity to search for software, skills, and save presentations or programs you have an interest in. If you have no idea where to begin, navigate the platform for what shows up on your LinkedIn Learning home page. Many of the content has been placed in different categories like trends, Editor's Picks, and learn within 30 minutes. All of these are tailored to keep your mind and skills as sharp as possible.

Constant education has no negative impact on you. Enhancing your knowledge and strengthening the skills you already have is vital to remaining a leader in your industry. By keeping up with the favorite topics, industry trends, and the moves your competitors are making, you will have more confidence in your capacity to support the needs and questions of your clients.

- Active Status: Platforms like Facebook have been capitalizing on this green dot to ensure users find it less challenging to interact with one another when they are online. Now, LinkedIn offers you the same feature. When you go to the profile page of one of your connections, you will see a green dot beside the photo of those that are active and online.

By knowing if someone is available and online, it enhances the possibility of them coming across your note and responding to it. The same applies when you have your active status set to be seen, so ensure it is turned on. To do this, use the following steps:

1. Head to the "Settings & Privacy" page which you can find underneath your photo.

2. In the Privacy page, navigate downwards till you get to the option which states: "How others see your LinkedIn activity."

3. Select "Manage active status" to ensure your connections can tell when you are online.

- Career Advice: If you are looking to begin a new career or to make a change to your present career, it can be of immense benefit to you if you get advice from someone experienced who has gone down a similar route. Career Advice helps connect you with other, more experienced professionals. If you do have the advice to give, you will also be connected to someone within your line of expertise.

You can see this as a method of online marketing, without the need to make a deal. You are certain to create connections this way if you use your experience and opinions in helping others. It can also assist you in the promotion of your brand without you selling actively.

- LinkedIn Publishing: This is a feature has existed for a while, but now, LinkedIn has made it less complicated for users to publish authentic content. Now, you can modify your posting settings to ensure anyone can view it, even those who have no LinkedIn account. What this means is that any of your published content can be seen by a higher number of individuals.

When you share content that shows your expertise and opinion, which can reach a broad range of users, you are beginning conversions, which may result in new business opportunities and connections. The ability to direct customers to content you published helps in enhancing your business credibility as well.

- Advanced Search: If you do a lot of online shopping, then you may have an idea of how tiring running a search might be, especially if you have to scroll through tons of search results. Great search platforms offer you various filters which you can use in screening your results. LinkedIn ensures that it is easier for you to locate a professional, company, or keyword by adding filters to show up the instant you put down a term in the search bar.

Filters ensure it is less challenging for prospective clients to find you if your profile is complete. If you can keep your information and account up-to-date, you will show up in numerous filters. We will be covering how to do this later in this book. Now that you know the features at your disposal, let us explore some of the benefits offered to you by LinkedIn.

Benefits of LinkedIn to your Marketing Strategy

Regardless of if you are running a new business or it is one that has been running for a long time, a good marketing plan can ensure you get the success you desire. A precious resource many businesses and marketers tend to ignore when putting together a marketing strategy is LinkedIn. In addition to expanding your network and increasing your clientele, LinkedIn can also connect you to people with the same business mind like you who can help you attain success.

Including LinkedIn to your marketing strategy can help bring about a successful enterprise. If you can run your LinkedIn account with skill and proficiency, you can make the platform work in achieving your needs. If you are still not convinced, below are a few of the benefits you stand to gain from creating and managing a profile on LinkedIn.

It Offers a Social Platform Which is Friendly to Your Business

As opposed to other platforms that transitioned to providing services for businesses, LinkedIn was established with professionals and companies in mind right from the start. It also has an algorithm which is not as complicated as other platforms like Instagram and Facebook. This aids in ensuring your presence and reach spreads further through your online community, while maintaining the right level of social interaction. LinkedIn is an excellent platform for resources and referrals, but still provides a personal presence which businesses require to be successful.

It is a Great Way to Find New Talent

Although career websites and job boards have been the leading platforms to locate capable job seekers, over the last four years, the use of social sites for professional networking has blown up over the previous four years. As stated by research done by LinkedIn, these platforms, including LinkedIn have experienced a 72 percent boost in its use for job recruitment, in comparison to a 15 percent enhancement for internet job boards and a 16 percent reduction for staffing agencies ("The Global Trends That Will Shape Recruiting In 2015 [INFOGRAPHIC]", 2014).

It Enhances Your Personal and Professional Credibility

LinkedIn is a platform that many businesses have not taken advantage of in comparison to other platforms. For instance, Facebook has more than 2 billion users (Yurieff, 2019), while LinkedIn has over 610 million users ("About LinkedIn", 2019). This proves that not many businesses are paying attention to LinkedIn as a Crucial Social Channel.

For businesses, this is terrific news because it provides an untapped platform which is not filled with too much competition. You can easily make yourself stand out from the others in your niche by posting content on your account three or more times weekly. It is vital to know that for this to work, the content on your personal page and business page must be thought-provoking, high quality, and consistent. When you upload posts using your business profile, you establish yourself as an expert in your niche. On the other hand, by making posts on your profile, you are developing a connection with your followers, which is more intimate, and may bring you more business in the long run.

It Can Push Traffic to Your Site

If you make frequent posts, you can add a link which redirects viewers to your site for additional information. According to research, Linked In's referral traffic to a website has more pages visited, a smaller bounce rate and more time on a site in comparison to other platforms. There are numerous ways to get traffic to your website, which include posting articles, information about a new product, articles, and a host of others. By developing and maintaining a presence on LinkedIn, you will enhance the credibility you have with your followers.

LinkedIn is an Efficient Platform to Launch Products

Social media platforms, especially LinkedIn, has made a lot of impact on the way we share product information and news to consumers, bloggers, and media. As stated by a Regalix poll, now LinkedIn is the leading platform for lots of B2B businesses. More than 80 percent of B2B companies reported that LinkedIn is the platform they utilize for product launches compared to 54 percent who utilize Facebook, and 71 percent who use Twitter (Tiwari, 2019).

It Can Enhance Physical Professional Relationships

LinkedIn can aid your business in nurturing and establishing vital relationships online. Nonetheless, it has been suggested by research that it can also assist in strengthening face-to-face connections. A Wishpond infographic states that 44 percent of the users on LinkedIn develop enhanced physical relationships through their utilization of the platform ("[INFOGRAPHIC] Q2 2013: The State of LinkedIn", 2013).

It Can Increase the Search Visibility of Your Brand

If you have a properly optimized company page and LinkedIn profile, it can help in enhancing your possibility of getting a high ranking in Google search. This can offer your business loads of benefits ranging from new opportunities and more sales.

To make sure you will rank in a search, ensure you are doing the following:

- Utilizing the appropriate keywords in your page description and bio

- Applying descriptive words in your company name and job title

- Fill up all the sections in your company description and your profile

- Incorporate links to your blog and site in your posts, profile, and descriptions.

Posts on LinkedIn Have the Possibility of Getting to all the Followers of Your Page

In comparison to other platforms, there is no filtered feed on LinkedIn. Any updates you make to your company page on LinkedIn shows up on the feeds of your followers. This applies regardless of how much engagement they have had with your posts previously. What this implies is that all of the labor you put into developing your page will provide you with a stable audience that is not restricted or screened by an algorithm.

However, this does not imply every one of your followers will be on LinkedIn when you make a post. Due to this, it is vital that your posts are regular to get the best reach. As stated by LinkedIn, businesses should aim to post 20 times or more each month if they aim to get to roughly 60 percent of their viewers ("The Sophisticated Guide to Marketing on LinkedIn", 2019).

It is the Most Effective Social Media Channel for Distributing Content

The Content Marketing Institute and MarketingProfs, carried out a study in 2014, which found out that 94 percent of B2B marketers utilize

LinkedIn in the distribution of their content (DeMers, n.d.). Also, the study found out that marketers pointed out LinkedIn as the most effective platform for distributing content, getting a better rank than Facebook, Twitter, and Google+.

When you share your content on LinkedIn, it gets it ahead of your present followers and connections. If you then use LinkedIn ads, it further spreads the reach by letting you target those who you distribute your content to, which could range from prospective clients to influencers in the industry.

Chapter 2

Creating a LinkedIn account

Using the LinkedIn platform requires an individual to set up a LinkedIn login. This is a small price that grants you access to a network of numerous professionals. To simplify the process of creating a LinkedIn login, the next section gives you a breakdown of the steps to take.

An account is vital to the development of a personal network. The growth of the personal network requires you to get other professionals on the platform to join. Self-promotion and business advertisements are some of the significant benefits of a vast network.

The sections that follow will give you a guide on how to create both a Login and a Business account on LinkedIn.

Steps to Setting up a LinkedIn Login

To implement the steps given, the first action you need to take is to open the website, LinkedIn.com, on your preferred web browser. Follow the steps below to create the Login:

Step 1

The first step is to provide your basic information. To do this, scroll to the Join Now button on the right side of the page. You are taken to a new page where you have to complete the requested information in four separate boxes as follows:

- The first box for your first name

- The second box for your last name

- The third box for your email address

- A password consisting of a minimum of six characters

To come up with a strong password, you should know that a combination of uppercase, lowercase, and either a special character or number is vital.

Step 2

Providing information pertaining to your location and employment status are the actions you need to take in completing this step. You can supply this information on the next screen.

The options available for employment status include:

- Employed

- Looking for Work

- Business Owner

- Working Independently

- A student

Depending on the option you select, the other fields will differ. For the Employed option, the other fields include Company, Country, Zip Code of your location, and Job Title.

The name of the business or Company name, Industry of business operations, zip code of your location, and country are the other details you need to input if you select the Business Owner option.

When you select Working Independently or Looking for work, in addition to the Country and Zip Code of your location, you need to provide an industry where you would like to work. Upon becoming a member, the profile edit option offers the opportunity to choose various industries if it suits your needs.

For those that pick A Student, you need to provide the College/University name, attendance dates, field of interest, Zip Code of your location, and country. When completing these fields, there are lists that pop-up as you begin typing. This helps to simplify the process.

Unless a user requests a premium account, there will be no request for a street address. Also, while LinkedIn displays your region, it ensures that the zip code remains private information.

Upon completion of the process, you can click Continue. To prevent issues in the future, you can go through the details you have provided to ensure that it is accurate.

Step 3

Unlike the previous steps, this is elective and at the discretion of the individual. It involves connecting your email to import contacts from the address book. The goal is to grow your network at a fast pace.

While you complete the process of the LinkedIn login setup, the email address import option is available. It assists in developing your contact list. By taking this step, the LinkedIn platform will aid you in scanning through your address book and identifying any email that is connected to a LinkedIn profile. You can then decide to invite these users to become a part of your network.

LinkedIn supports the use of different forms of email. Here are some of the acceptable options:

- AOL

- Yahoo mail

- Gmail

- Hotmail

- Other

The 'Other' option provides a list of email services that don't appear in the original selections list. Therefore, you still have the opportunity to import contacts if you use the lesser known email services. Regardless of the option you select, access to your address book by the LinkedIn platform is only possible if you log in to the email account.

There are certain things you need to remember when using this option. The first is that it is optional. This means that you can decide to go to the next stage without going through the process by simply clicking on the 'Skip this step' link.

You should also understand that in some cases, an email may not match a user you are sure is on the platform. One simple reason is that some individuals may use a different email address to join the LinkedIn platform.

The appearance of a confirmation screen is the next stage after you accept or skip the email address import. This screen informs you of the delivery of a confirmation email to your email address. This is the address you used to register on the platform.

For some of the popular email services, there is a button that redirects to the login page of your email provider to ease the process.

The confirmation message you are expecting may take a few minutes to deliver, or it might come in immediately. The time it takes doesn't matter. The crucial part is that you perform the following actions when you receive it:

- Click on the confirmation message from LinkedIn

- Input your login details to access your LinkedIn profile

- Take your first step towards connecting to a network of professionals

Now that you have learned how to create a personal account on LinkedIn let us have a look at how to create a Company page or account.

Creating a LinkedIn Company Account

A company page is another vital aspect of the LinkedIn platform. It offers a number of benefits to individuals that run a business which makes it very difficult to overlook for anyone looking to get the best out of the platform.

It is necessary you prepare several things before you begin the process. These include graphics such as logo as well as the right to engage in the company page creation.

This guide will put you through the process, but you should know that a LinkedIn profile that is active is a prerequisite for a company page.

Step 1

Creating a Company Page is quite straightforward if you know where to look. To begin the process, move to the upper right corner to find the "Work" tab. Clicking on this tab opens a list, and you can find the option to "Create a Company Page" at the bottom. Locate the plus (+) sign and click on it.

Premium member or not, any personal account is suitable for the process of setting up a company page. The only thing worthy of note is that an active account with complete details is essential. You may have to wait a few weeks to create a company page if you set up a new account for this purpose.

Step 2

The next step in this process is to supply all the essential details of your business. This is the page that you land on after choosing to create a company page. The first detail is the business name. Here, you have the option of switching the title case, so be sure to make the name an exact match of how the LinkedIn company page should display the name.

The business URL is the detail you need to input in the second box. To simplify the process, the LinkedIn platform will input your company name automatically into this box. There will be a dash between the words that complete the company name. You have the option of editing this name to something more straightforward and cohesive with your brand.

For the sake of simplicity, you may need to delete the dashes to form a single word or use a URL that matches those on other social media platforms like Facebook. Consider a company with Cabe Data Research as the name. The automatic URL input by the LinkedIn platform will appear as, linkedin.com/company/cabe-data-research.

You can edit and simplify the URL to appear as, linkedin.com/cabedataresearch.

An acronym that you use to represent the business in your marketing campaigns is also suitable for creating a URL. This is a much shorter URL that anyone can quickly recollect, but its use depends on the availability of the URL.

The last action you need to take is to offer a form of verification to show that you have the authority and as proof that you are an official representative of the company.

The option to create a University page is also available. This option offers some additional features like the alumni section of the page. Qualification to create a University page is at the discretion of LinkedIn. It is necessary you reach out to LinkedIn if you intend to set up this page.

Step 3

This step involves improving the appearance of the page to show the connection with the company. You are merely going to be branding your business page. This is not a step that you can overlook since the company name is the only detail that connects the LinkedIn page with your company.

The cover image is the first thing you set up. A quick tip; avoid any cover image that includes a text or word. The reason is that the display of the cover image varies when you login to LinkedIn on a desktop or mobile. A size of 1536 X 768 is perfect for the cover image. Remember, the goal is to brand the page to match your business so, the image should be a visual representation of everything about your business.

Your business logo is the next graphic you should add. With a size of 300 x 300 px, adding a text would be useless since it would be difficult to read at this size. If at this point, you have not decided on the logo for your business, the picture of the founder can suit this purpose. For the best results, a square logo is necessary.

If your business doesn't have a logo at this point, you should try making the most of a personal profile for a while.

Step 4

Providing a description of your company is the next step you should take. Any potential client needs to know about the business and what it can offer. Don't take this step lightly, anyone considering interaction with your company as a client or employee will use this page as a means of assessment.

If you want to give an in-depth description of your company, you get up to 2,000 words for this purpose. Notwithstanding, a short description is often the best. To get straight to the point in your description, you can answer the following questions:

- What objectives do I want to achieve using this page?

- Who is my primary target audience? Are they potential clients, employees, or job seekers?

- What unique features can make my company stand out?

- What benefits does the company offer?

This step requires patience. You don't rush into creating a description. You can meet with other individuals within the company to get multiple inputs with varying perspectives.

A proofreader is also crucial once you complete the description. This individual will check through for errors you may have overlooked.

Upon completion of the about section, making a selection of specialties is the next action. You have the option of picking up to 20 of these specialties. It is essential that the specialties you pick mirror the strengths of your business.

You don't have to select all 20 now, and you can adopt new specialties later as the business progresses.

Step 5

Here, all you need to do is add the crucial details regarding your company. The details you need to include are as follows:

- Company size

- Year founded

- Website

- Industry

- Location

- Company type

For a company that has set up shop in various locations, there is the option of selecting one main office during the setup.

Step 6

During the setup of a company page, the option to connect groups to the page is available. The groups you connect to can be those you own, or those that you feel will have a positive impact on your target audience. It is crucial you pick groups that offer high-quality content.

Step 7

There are other options that you can access on the page. You can address these options after publishing the page. The possibility of including a tagline becomes visible while you can also choose a call to action for the company page you create.

You can select from any of the following options when setting up a call to action:

- Learn more

- Sign up

- Contact us

- Visit website

- Register

You can make the most of the call to action feature by inputting a URL that can ease the process of directing users to a conversion funnel on your website.

Step 8: Content Creation

Like all other social platforms, content creation is also a crucial aspect of the LinkedIn platform. Your first post can be a short video with a focus on an aspect of your company. Aside from the video option, you can upload your content in a text or image format.

The growth of the company page depends on the frequency of your uploads. Based on the industry of your company, you can get useful tips on the best content to upload using a tool on the platform.

Ensure that your posts follow a schedule by making use of a scheduling software or tool online.

Subscribing for a LinkedIn Premium Account

The LinkedIn premium account uses a paid plan that offers an upgrade from the free version. This upgrade comes with numerous benefits that make it worth the price. There is a one-month free trial available to any user that decides to upgrade to the premium services.

The payment of a subscription fee begins at the expiration of the free trial period. Payments can be monthly or annually, and this is dependent on the premium account type. Some of the essential features that you obtain once you become a premium member include:

- Unlimited Open Link messages

- Premium search filters and better search functionality

- Premium content access

- Open Link Membership

- InMail credits and message

- View users that open your profile

- Reference search option

- Replies to your questions within a business day

There are other benefits such as a LinkedIn badge beside your name, improved communication options, a look at your viewership, and many more.

Depending on your profession, there are four main premium accounts you can select from. These include the following:

- Recruiter Lite

- Job Seeker

- Business Plus

- Sales Navigator

Below, we will explore each of these in detail.

Recruiter Lite:

The LinkedIn Recruiter platform offers the option of the Recruiter Lite, which offers a low cost with scaled-down operations. The Recruiter Lite offers a premium feature at a monthly price. The purpose of the Recruiter Lite is to enable businesses to search for skilled individuals and recruit them at a much faster speed.

The interface design of the Recruiter Lite also focuses on simplifying the staffing workflow. There is job slot management, targeted search, and administrative functions that simplify user accounts management; there is also InMail management, profile management that includes project folders, and other productivity and collaborative features.

There is no restriction to the access you gain through the LinkedIn Recruiter Lite. It offers 30 InMail messages for each month and each member of the team. You can use this in communicating with professionals directly with the InMail feature.

There are lots of other excellent features available such as reporting and analytics tools that enable you to monitor the activities of team members. The search results provide access to unlimited profiles as well as a suggested profiles feature that goes to the 3rd degree. Find some of the top candidates for a position through the use of the advanced search filters while the dynamic suggestions help in the expansion of your talent pool. These are all features with a focus on improving the simplicity of the recruiting process.

Job Seeker:

The Job Seeker version is suitable for any individual that is on the LinkedIn platform in search of jobs. Requirements for users may vary, but the account requires a monthly payment. Certain features are open to users of this account.

Some of the features include the option to find out your profile viewers over 90 days, communication with recruiters through direct messages, and profile comparison with other candidates for a job. Your profile also appears as the top or featured applicant anytime an employer uses the search tool. For the InMail feature, you receive 5 per month while there is a credit back if you don't get an InMail response within seven days.

To show that you are in search of a job, you get the option of placing a badge on your LinkedIn profile. This makes it more visible to employers. To meet more professionals, you receive 15 introductions through which you can meet the connections of users that make up your connections.

Following the SEO tactics that Google implements, this account also makes it to the first page or sometimes, the top of the search results. Since most people don't usually take the time to move on to the next page, you can benefit greatly from this improvement in ranking. Both free users and premium users typically find a box that indicates the number of users that have viewed their profile on the right side of the page. For premium users, more detailed information is available by clicking on this box.

Business Plus:

As a professional, there is always a need to grow your network and engage with other professionals. To achieve these objectives, the Business Plus offers an excellent solution. You pay a monthly fee before getting access to search results with an unlimited number of profiles, twenty-five introductions, and suggested profiles up to the 3rd degree. You also receive 15 InMails every month along with a seven-day response guarantee. With a maximum number of 30 credits, your unused email credits will roll over at the start of every month.

You can assess your performance by comparing your rank with your connections. This is available through unique prompts on your news feed. The performance of your connections is also visible through updates that are made available to you. You can also see an overview of your performance assessment over the last month.

Sales Navigator:

If you want to improve your sales targeting, then this is the account to use. LinkedIn integrates the Sales Navigator with the technology from Point Drive. Combining data-derived insights with the massive database available, sales professionals have a better chance of meeting prospective buyers or companies that require their services through the enhanced targeting feature.

Automatic import of appropriate accounts is available through CRM data integration. More features are present, and they all come after you pay a monthly fee.

The Sales Navigator Tool is essential to the productivity of sales reps. Using this tool, it is possible to monitor their conversations and safely transfer them to an offline platform. The offline platform is usually to promote the conversation or include the prospects into a sales process. Through the combination of sales with social channels, LinkedIn assures connections of a form of credibility.

Using your history as a guide, you also receive lead contacts recommendations from LinkedIn. Another useful information you receive is an update on the decision makers working with contacts on your list. The importance of these updates is to be sure that for each company, the user you are communicating with is the top decision maker.

To enhance targeting options, accounts updates can be filtered based on general contact updates, company updates, and content shares. Sales professionals find these features crucial in ensuring they are well-informed on the actions of their contacts.

Other features of this account include larger background images and headshots.

Selecting a LinkedIn premium service is dependent on your profession or business. What you intend to achieve on the LinkedIn platform also affects this decision. To get a good grip on what a premium account offers, you should take advantage of the free trial period.

Making a Payment

To make a payment, you must first input your LinkedIn password for account verification. The next step is to choose a method of payment, and this can be through a PayPal account or Credit Card. Depending on your choice, you will need to fill in your details.

You can then learn about the features of any plan you select by clicking on the "Start your free trial" button that is available. If you don't like the features the plan offers, ensure you cancel the plan before the completion of the free trial period to prevent the platform from charging.

A receipt is sent to your email while a printable receipt pops up on the screen. To close this page, click on the "I'm done" button.

Chapter 3

How to Create a LinkedIn Profile

That Sells

Your LinkedIn profile is the first thing your buyer sees when he/she comes across your page. This implies that your profile can create a first impression about you to the buyer. Many marketers take their profiles as an after-thought, and this is where the problem lies for a lot of them. If you don't put in adequate effort to write your profile from the eyes of the buyer, they may not take a second glance at you. Your profile can have a positive or negative effect on your brand, and it can have an impact on your capacity to sell to your target buyers.

In essence, you can't make your profile seem like a resume, except you are in search of a job, then that is fine. However, if you are a marketer who wants to sell, you must explicitly state it to your potential buyer that you understand the issues they are dealing with and can help them solve it. Your profile has to be detailed enough to convert viewers to buyers, which will, in turn, bring you sales. If you are unable to have conversions with your ideal buyers, you will be unable to sell more right? You need to understand that your LinkedIn profile is vital to being successful in selling. LinkedIn is the best platform to develop a network for business professionals. However, it would be pointless if your profile does not draw in new leads or sales. A good profile will ensure your buyers find you, grow to trust that you can offer them a solution, and reach out to you to ensure you get those sales conversions.

In this chapter, we will explore how you can optimize your LinkedIn profile to help you boost your sales game to where it needs to be. Having covered why your profile is vital for helping you make sales, let us first take a look at some fundamental components your profile must have for it to bring in sales.

Basic Components of a LinkedIn profile

For your profile to function as a true sales asset, it needs to have the following vital elements:

- A profile picture, preferably a recent one. You need to note that this is not just a social platform for connecting with your friends, but business professionals. So, don't use a picture of you at a party; instead, go with a headshot. Ensure you have a smile on your face, which will ensure those who view your page feel great about connecting with you.

- A background banner that represents your brand and explicitly lets viewers know where you work.

- An appealing headline that draws in buyers because it summarizes how you can be of help to them.

- Relevant media like audio, video, presentations, among others, that further show your buyers how you can assist them.

- A profile summary which plays the role of a narrative further elaborating on how you can assist your buyers. It should also offer them some insights to you as an individual.

The above are the basic components that need to be included in a LinkedIn profile, which changes it to a profile that is all about the buyer. Including these will help you attract visits from more buyers and enhance the possibility of getting more sales conversions.

Does Your Profile Really Help Bring More Sales?

The simple answer to this is YES!

The truth is, if you want to appeal to more prospects, develop a pipeline and increase your sales, you need to make the vital steps to exploit all of the features LinkedIn makes available to you. To attract buyers, it is crucial for you to position yourself as a person that can help find solutions to the distinct issues they are facing.

The way you develop your profile, with the help of content through the perspective of your buyer, in addition to how you interact with people, will ensure they want to know you further. With your profile, you can position yourself as someone vital who can assist your buyer.

The type of content you upload on LinkedIn can ensure your buyers find you, and nudge them to start a conversation with you (We will be covering more of these in the chapters to follow).

The more you place yourself out there using content relevant to your buyers, request a connection, or join a conversation, the more you develop opportunities for yourself to be spotted and contacted by buyers.

And that leads to people getting to your profile. So how do you ensure your profile is in place for these visitors? Let's take a look at a few strategies that might help.

Write Your Profile from The Perspective of the Buyer

For many marketers and salespersons, the profile is a place to write about their careers and all about the things they have achieved, without anything that offers no value to the buyer. This should not be the way to go because buyers have no interest in all of that because it is "You-Focused" rather than "Buyer-Focused."

A prospective client does not want to collaborate with you because of how you surpassed your target years ago or how great at negotiations you are. No, instead, they want to collaborate because you have a capacity to provide solutions to a problem their business is facing, help them make more profit or cut down on expenses, or finish up a project they are stuck on. Ultimately, your buyer is only interested in learning how you can make their life easier and better than it is presently.

Your LinkedIn profile should let your customers know how you can help them, and should not be a resume of your accomplishments. For the perspective of sales, your focus should be on how you are a resource. It should not be about promotion.

Integrate an Amazing Headshot Image

Like we covered earlier, your profile picture has to be a professional headshot. Any photo you decide to go with needs to be right for business. This means a picture of you at your friend's birthday party won't work here. Same applies with a picture of you at a bar. Instead, it has to be one that shows your professional side, and more importantly, it has to be a recent one. Ensure that any picture you go with is the same way you look if someone decides to have a physical meeting with you.

Using a logo is not ideal, because LinkedIn has to do with branding you as a person, and not a company. But a more important reason why this is not advisable is that it does not go with the user agreement of LinkedIn.

Worse still, if you plan to attract buyers, stay away from empty profiles.

Many buyers love to see who they will be working with. Also, it has been proven that profiles with a great photo have a 40% increase in InMail responses and 11 times more views as opposed to LinkedIn profiles without pictures (Osman, 2019).

A few helpful tips to note when taking a profile picture include:

- Have a smile which shows your teeth

- Let your eyes be focused on the camera

- The image should cover your head to shoulders. You can also decide to go with a head to waist framing.

Having taken note of that, below are a few things not to do:

- Do not put on sunglasses

- Stay away from complete body shots

- Don't use a dark background or clothing colors

- Don't stare away from the camera

Also, smiling is essential. Whatever you do, you need to remember to smile. When you have a warm smile on your face, those who come across your page will be more keen on becoming a part of your network.

Lastly, your background banner is vital. It is a straightforward way of highlighting your brand on LinkedIn. If you work alongside a company, after getting the needed permission, you can integrate the brand, fonts, colors, and logo of your organization into your header.

Use a Great Headline

Your headline has to be one that encourages the viewer/reader to see more. It is a strategy used by lots of news blogs on the internet. Your headline is the initial information about you that your prospective buyer will read. For this reason, it needs to count. This means you have to write a headline that will URGE them to read more, and learn about you and how you, and the services you provide, could be of benefit to them in solving their business issues.

Your headline, picture, and name will be displayed on most of your interactions with other users of LinkedIn, so you need to put in more effort to ensure it works correctly for you.

Many marketers make the error of not putting a lot of time into their headlines. They don't describe what they do, who they are, and where they work. Your headline is an excellent location to take advantage of keywords. Use keywords for the services you will like your prospects to find you for, while elaborating on what you do and whom you do it for.

Your profile headline demonstrates how you can be of assistance and who you are in 120 characters or lower. Also, if possible, you can add the name of your company in your headline too.

Below are a few things you should ensure your profile headline does:

- Consists of Keywords

- Points out your Target Audience

- Displays the name of your organization

- Tells your prospective clients how you can help

120 characters may seem too limited for you to incorporate all of these, but it is possible. Below is an example:

"Assisting Financial Institutions in Western Canada to Mitigate Cyber Attacks | Veco Industries."

In your headline, try to explicitly state the individuals you can help, if applicable, the way you can help them, the organization you work for and the geographical location you can help. Your final goal is to aid your prospective buyer, which implies you need to consider them at every moment. They want a solution to the problems they are dealing with in their business. By ensuring your profile headline offers that information, you will draw more attention to yourself and get more appointments because potential clients will understand what you do, who you are, and how you can help them. Increase in appointments means an increase in your chances for more sales.

Let Your Profile Summary Tell an Excellent Story

This is sometimes called the background section, and it is a vital aspect of your profile. You will get 2000 characters to summarize in detail what you do, whom you work for, and who you are. If you aim to get more conversions, you have to ensure this segment is about your audience.

Here, you need to highlight your relevance to your reader further. It is not a necessity for it to be about your achievements or the number of years you have spent in the field. Using SEO here is critical, but something even more significant is the story you tell your audience from your summary alongside the insights you offer. A profile which is buyer-focused will help you develop credibility and trust.

Here, you want to further elaborate on what you do and how you can be of help. You need to be yourself and not what you believe anyone else needs you to be. The more you tell your story with the buyer in mind, the less challenging it will be for visitors to understand how you can serve them better and the higher the possibility of converting them into actual clients.

Ensure you emphasize the needs and wants of your audience. If you fail to focus on their areas of duress and let them know you are a valuable resource to them, you will not be an appealing choice for them to get help.

Most times, buyers use LinkedIn in the same way they utilize Google. They look for solutions to problems. If you capitalize on the appropriate keywords and place them strategically, your summary page will come up more when people run searches on LinkedIn. You need to make your summary page SEO optimized so your prospects can locate you when they run a search.

Your Grammar Matters

This is a platform for professionals, and your goal is to find buyers. What this means is, you need to make sure your profile does not have any punctuation, spelling, and grammatical errors. Errors can make your prospects believe you have no attention to detail, and you are careless. If you don't put the needed time into this, the individuals viewing your page will assume you are someone who is careless and lazy, which is not right for any business.

Buyers are interested in someone who pays attention to details. The reason is that it proves that you care and to them, this means you care about them, what they want as well as their organization. They are interested in knowing what you can offer them, and if they believe you can't represent them in a positive light, then they will move to the profile of someone else who can.

You have to do ensure that all you write has a purpose, and it connects. Your profile plays the role of a funnel, so you need to make sure you have an appealing buyer-focused profile that progresses naturally, and urges the reader to perform a specific action as they go through your profile. This could be to urge them to contact you, or lead them to your landing page or site, or connect with you.

A great profile draws the viewer to the headline. An excellent headline then navigates them to the summary, which is properly developed and buyer focused, directs the viewer to your experience, where he/she will find out more about the specifics of what you can do to assist them.

The goal is to ensure they take action, and no viewer will take action from a profile not correctly written and riddled with errors.

You also need to ensure you speak your buyer's language. Don't forget that you are showcasing how you can provide solutions to their problems. You also want to bear in mind that your profile is not a way to show your achievements or how amazing you are. It should urge people to want to learn on their own. You are a person that is relevant to them, someone who can solve their problems. This is what your profile should show.

Add Media

Using media that demonstrates your value will further prove your credibility and skill to the buyer. You want to make sure to include any relevant videos or presentations which you can upload on your URL. This is a better option than uploading files because once you add a link, it is easier to update to more recent files as opposed to uploading videos. Any individual can say he is excellent at something, but when you showcase previous samples of how you can assist them, then you go further in proving any attention the prospective client gives you, is worth it.

If you work with one, you can request media from your marketing department. If you have your brand, you can get your presentations. A great location to display media is your profile summary; then, you can upload on your Experience Section, which allows you to accentuate media that has to do with that position. It is beneficial if your content demonstrates your problem-solving process and how you are of value to your present clients and prospective clients. Media is a core item to attract prospective clients because it helps you develop credibility instantly. It also lets buyers see how much value you can offer them without any hassles.

Make your Experience Section Comprehensive

In the Experience Section, you can place more emphasis on what you do and who you are. Here, you are provided with 2000 characters to say what your organization is about and what you do there. You can outline features, services, and unique selling points (USPs) in this section. You outline what makes you and your organization stand out from others, offering the same services as you.

You can link the LinkedIn page of your company, so their logo appears here. If you don't do this, you may be left with an empty square beside your info which does not seem professional. If you don't have the logo of your company on display, the prospective client may begin to doubt you as they may be imagining the kind of organization you work with that has no LinkedIn company logo. If you aim to place yourself in the same category with the top leaders in your field, then you need to make sure the presence of your organization can be seen in this section.

When putting the Experience Section of your LinkedIn profile together, below are a few things you want it to consist of:

- Description of your present job: What you do, who you are, How you can be of assistance.

- Description of your prior jobs: The roles you played and how you were of help

- Media: even if the media was from a role you previously played, it does not matter as it helps in search and establishing your authority and credibility.

For each role, pay attention to the needs and wants of the audience and how you satiated them. All of your work descriptions have to be buyer-focused and accentuate how you were an indispensable resource to your client.

Consider The Policies

When putting your profile in place, you don't want to include anything that goes against the communication policies of your organization or include anything misleading and untrue. If you place a specific employer as your current job, you need to be certain that you are not going against any of their policies as you may pay a very high price.

You want to rest assured with the knowledge that you have a compliant LinkedIn profile, so you can pay more attention to getting buyers.

Don't Leave Any Open Fields

Complete LinkedIn profiles are the best profiles. The reason is simple: 50 percent of buyers stay away from sales experts that have no complete profile. The following sections are some you need to fill in, which will aid you in attracting new prospects and ensure they go further in conversion:

- Education: Regardless of the degree you have, you want it to be on your profile. It does not matter if you did not attend a prestigious university, as it is an aspect of who you are. You are provided with 2000 characters to speak about your activities in school and how they helped in defining you. Also, this could be something you share in common with a customer or business partner, which could lead to new connections.

- Skills: Your skills are vital, and you need to outline them. When you put your skills here, you are privy to endorsements and the more the number of these you amass, the more credible you seem to prospects. What's more, each endorsement you include ensures it is less difficult to locate your profile under that skill or keyword. You can add as much as 50 skills in your profile, and only you can add those suitable to you. If you fail to include your skills, it will be added by LinkedIn, so you want to ensure you do it yourself.

- Endorsements: Endorsements share a lot of similarities with the "like" you get on Facebook, but this does not mean they serve no purpose. Outline your skills and endorse some of the people you know. Be sure to put on the endorse feature to be able to do this.

- Recommendations: This area of your profile can offer you lots of benefits. To begin, write genuine recommendations for those you previously worked alongside. This could include your present and past clients, colleagues, and bosses. Selectively contact those you have worked alongside to ask for a recommendation politely. You can direct them to pay attention to some skills of your choosing. The recommendation segment of your profile can be indexed by search engines like Yahoo, Google, and Bing. When this occurs, when people run searches you using the keywords in your recommendations, you can be found. For a marketer, this can be a very significant tool because when a buyer searches for the services you offer on purpose, and contact you, they have a 5-6 times higher possibility of converting. It also proves why recommendations can be of great benefit.

Your Profile Is Vital to Your Sales Success

If you want to be successful in selling on LinkedIn, you need to pay attention to your profile. Doing it the right way can bring you a ton of sales down the road.

Chapter 4

Determining Your Ideal Customers

By now, you understand how the platform works for connecting you with professionals. You also know that if you hit the right buttons, you can find users who can convert to buyers for your business. However, for many marketers, the issue lies in determining their ideal customers on the platform. Many add their friends and family members and later find out that these set of users have no interest in the services or products they offer. The truth is before you can make a sale or conversion, you need to determine your ideal clients and target them specifically. That way, your possibility of conversion is much higher. How then do you do this? In this chapter, we will be looking into a few strategies that can help you do this efficiently. The first step you have to take is to make a profile of your ideal client.

Create A Profile of Your Ideal Client

Similar to the various strategies, it is essential for you to plan. In this situation, you have to determine who your ideal client is first before you begin to try selling the product or services you offer.

To help you out with this, consider your main products and services and ask yourself the following questions:

- What kind of users will be willing to spend cash on these specific products and services?

- Who requires the specific services I offer?

- Who will be keen on paying the rate you set in place for those services?

Your answers to these questions will take you one step further to finding you're the best client for your services. The next thing you need to do is to ask yourself about the best demographic for your ideal client. Do this by asking yourself the following questions:

- Do you want to work with a group, company, or individual?

- What country do they need to reside in for you to be able to cater to them or work with their schedule like time, city, etc.?

- What age bracket do your ideal clients fall into?

When you have determined all of these, you can move on to the next step of putting it all together.

Put it together

Now, you need to combine the major services you provide, along with the profile of your ideal client to locate your target market. Do not forget that the level of detail you use here will determine how clear your image will be of the users you should be targeting when trying to pitch your services.

For instance: let's say you are a brand expert, who lives in New Jersey and can only offer services to clients from 4.00pm – 1.00am EST.

The next step it to do an analysis of your ideal client profile and core services. Based on your expertise, you learn that your ideal client is a company in Australia. Researching further can help you point out various cities where you can begin your search for clients.

Be realistic when going through this process. There is no need to rush this process. After you have fully determined this, you can now move on to putting a list of companies or individuals together.

List Out the Organizations or Individuals You Would Like to Collaborate with

After you have determined your targets, the next step is to create your important keywords. Then run a search using the LinkedIn search bar and list out the users and companies that your services may be suitable for. Searching via google can also be of help here. When a list of companies come up, you can find out if they have a page on LinkedIn and try to establish a connection with them.

Establishing Connection

Before establishing a connection with the individuals or company you feel will be ideal clients for your business, first check out "How You're Connected" to find out if there are any 1st, 2nd or 3rd-degree connections. If you find any, find out if you have a personal relationship with any of these people. If so, reach out to them via LinkedIn or a call and request an introduction. You can also try to learn if he/she knows the decision maker in the organization.

If you have no close connections to the individual or company, take a look at all the users following the updates of the company. There is a high possibility that many users who work in the company will be following the updates. If you find a suitable candidate, you can use that in establishing a connection with the company you are targeting.

Using Common Ground to Find Your Ideal Clients

Another method of finding your ideal client is to locate common ground. Simply put, you look for users who share the same interest as you do. Perhaps they work in a sector similar to yours? Or maybe they work in a company that you are sure will benefit from the services or products you are offering.

You can also check out the schools they attended, and you may see something to use for a connection. The same is also applicable if you both follow the same group related to your niche. If so, you can already tell that he is interested in that industry and would most likely have an interest in the services or products you have on offer.

Marketing to Your Ideal Clients Successfully

After finding your ideal client and creating a connection with them, your objective is to become an authority and expert in your field in order to convert them to actual buyers.

You can do this by posting content consistently, in a way that your audience favors the most, like articles, images, videos, webinars, among others, all of which should be relevant to them.

Also, leave comments on their updates, respond to their comments as fast as you can, to keep them engaged, and build trust. If you do this the right way, you will be able to develop a loyal audience who will be keen to buy from you when the time comes.

Finding Your Niche on LinkedIn

Many people see LinkedIn as a social network strictly for professionals and nothing more. For this reason, lots of people, including marketers, don't know that LinkedIn offers a means of connecting to prospective clients because of the focus of the platform on b2b networking and job seeking.

However, LinkedIn is focused on creating links between individuals in particular sectors, which is reasonable from the perspective of a niche market. The platform has already been designed to make it less challenging for you to connect with entrepreneurs, industry leaders, organizations, and clients in your precise niche.

In this section, we will be learning how to find your niche on LinkedIn and how you can establish a connection with them.

Seeking Out Your Niche On LinkedIn

Follow Influencers Specific to Your Industry

Some years back, 'LinkedIn Today' was launched by LinkedIn, which was an RSS reader that drew in content from the entire user base of LinkedIn and displayed only information that was of relevance to your sector, or any topics you customized for the feed to send you. However, in the early part of 2013, LinkedIn bought the well-known feed app known as Pulse, which has taken over LinkedIn Today.

Using the LinkedIn Pulse, you have the choice of customizing your newsfeed using the following:

- Channels

- Publishers

- Influencers

Although it may be a great choice to look for your niche in all of the categories, the best place to check is the influencers category. When you locate influencers who are relevant to your selected niche in the huge list offered by pulse, you will be privy to subjects that are categorized as vital to your niche. You will also be privy to individuals who have something to do with your niche in a similar light. The possibility is that individuals who put in a similar amount of effort and time as you did, to involve themselves with niche influencers the same way you did, would probably be great options for your marketing and targeted networking.

Locate Niche-Relevant Groups with The Help of Targeted Keyword Searches

Another easy way to locate individuals within your niche is by using keyword searches on the search bar offered by LinkedIn. The search bar connects you with companies, individuals, and groups. When you input topics that have to do with your group, you have the chance of connecting with tons of people who are devoted and connected to your niche.

Launch Direct Connections

Lastly, instead of going through the processes above, you can just contact those in your niche directly. The first method is by sending a request to connect, which we covered earlier.

The second method is to use the **'people you may know'** option. This is a page created by LinkedIn consisting of individuals you share a connection with via other contacts, or you are in similar groups. Here, you can directly connect to people without the need to explain why you want to connect.

LinkedIn is a tool that can be very powerful for locating your ideal clients. When you do, you will learn that you will be more successful in selling your products and services if you pay attention to your ideal clients, determining what is vital to them and issues they are battling within their businesses. With the information you get from these, you can connect to them and help them achieve their needs while making sales in the process. It's a win-win situation.

Chapter 5

Best LinkedIn practices

LinkedIn stands as a behemoth, as it is the biggest social network platform for colleagues and professionals. While other sites such as Twitter, Instagram, and Facebook link you to a variety of people, LinkedIn connects your professional content and social connections to individuals that share your views.

You and your business can take advantage of this social media platform by simply following its best practices. LinkedIn is an excellent space for those that want to foster audiences, create communities, and promote content that correlates directly to your industry participants. This does not mean these things cannot be done on other social media platforms; however, LinkedIn is the most effective place for a business to build its professional community. In this chapter, we will be looking into some of the best practices you can adapt, as well as mistakes and how to avoid them. But first, why are these practices vital?

Why LinkedIn Best Practices Are Important

Considering there are over 3 million business pages available on LinkedIn ("About LinkedIn", 2019), it is a smart decision to use the social network for advertising your services and products, while also increasing your business development. When you effectively use this channel, you can create customer advocates, reach and engage new audiences, as well as users on diverse professional interests. LinkedIn can increase the memberships or customer base of a business or group.

This is done via engagement and community building. Businesses and marketers always attempt to create social interactions in ways that will achieve meaningful results.

The following LinkedIn best practices should be incorporated and then followed to give you the best chance to transform your social network platform into one that is an effective yet professional marketing tool.

Understand The Content Type to Post

A great reason to have your business on LinkedIn is to publish content. Content on social media is basically about your target audience and how you can channel your target audience towards the marketing funnel. When it comes to publishing content on LinkedIn, there are numerous caveats to be known. Below are a couple of content types that are known to be especially effective on LinkedIn:

Clickable Content: This content type has to be enticing, engaging, and it should make the reader want to read through to the next page. In the digital marketing world, clicks are what matter, as your content should be able to push readers to click for more with the right motivation.

A way to achieve this is to include visual content. Research has shown that users on LinkedIn are eleven times more likely to click or read an article if it contains a photo ("14 LinkedIn Hacks That Will Triple the Size of Your Network in Two Weeks", 2017). These stats are proof that visuals are the primary driver of content on LinkedIn, which is why there is no point pushing out content that is only plain text. It is also imperative that your content has the right call to action placed in it. If your audience is not asked to start a trial or click to read more, you are likely to see little to no movement. You have to make use of call to action phrases that are bound to convert.

Audience Specific: Of every single LinkedIn best practice, one very vital one is creating content that targets a specific audience. This translates to you developing content on LinkedIn that people in your chosen industry will want to read. To understand better of what your audience make up is you have to ask a couple of questions like:

- Who reads the content? You have to understand what your target audience is. You should know the type of people that click on your page and how you can direct your content to them.

- Who are your LinkedIn followers? Have a look at your followers so you can understand who your core demographics are.

- Who do I target? You have to find out the people you can use your content to target and work according to your campaign on LinkedIn.

Pique Interests: You should publish content that gives insights, discusses topics, and asks questions within your chosen industry to pique the interests of your readers. As soon as you figure out your audience and how you can make them click on your content, it is crucial to make sure that they continue reading. You should attempt to publish on LinkedIn content that asks pertinent and industry relevant questions. Your readers should be able to see that you are aware of your field. You shouldn't be shy. You should be willing to provide insights into the industry or show your readers a behind the scenes glimpse. It is vital that your readers continue reading your content.

Industry Events: Considering that LinkedIn is the biggest professional social media network, it makes great sense to publish content on forthcoming industry events to ensure that some conversations keep going. This social media platform comes with group channels which you can either create or join in regards to a particular event. It is on this group channel that you can discuss, engage, and offer up concerning where your company would be during an event. If you happen to be part of an industry that has sparse events to cover, you can make use of your

LinkedIn to promote and support causes. This is particularly great is your business prides itself on particular causes and matters, as LinkedIn is a great way to push out content which promotes not just the cause but your brand as well.

Visually Appealing: As mentioned earlier, visuals are essential in driving LinkedIn engagement. What this means is that the header image you pick should be one that is attractive, rather than just putting a stock photo of business people smiling. You can make use of uniquely free stock images sites; however, you have to ensure that your audience is not bored and your visuals must be engaging and sensible. If the aim is to promote a particular visual like an infographic, and your business does not have a graphic design team, there are other options you can use. Sites such as Piktochart and Canva can be used to create the image you require. You don't have to worry about creativity as LinkedIn is not Instagram where you are judged on looks. The most important category that is judged is that your infographic is informative and practical.

Career Angle: Since LinkedIn is a professional social network, you should feel free to publish content that has a career angle. You should provide users with insight into your industry and business, how the different teams work, as well as how it would be to work under you. LinkedIn is a perfect medium for corporate environment stories, as well as an avenue to create links to openings. When you add a career angle, you make it much easier for your vacancies to be quickly located.

Inspire Your Employees to Post Branded Content

You should understand that your employees can become your brand's most prominent ambassadors. So it makes sense to make use of their social powers to promote your brand, especially on a professional social network such as LinkedIn. Nevertheless, some employees might be a tad nervous about posting company content on their private social media handles. A study has shown that there are many reasons as to why

60

employees appear hesitant to post company content, media, or news, and they are:

- 21.6% of employees do not believe their employees would want them to post company content

- 15.7% of employees are not sure what to share.

- 77.3% of employees don't feel inspired to post company news on their social media ("The Deep Disconnect: An HR Data Report", n.d.)

While your employees feel like this, your business loses out on maximizing its reach and audience. Smart brands have discovered methods to encourage their employees to post content on platforms like LinkedIn. This ensures that their brand gains increased visibility. Below are a couple of reasons as to why it is imperative that your employees share:

- 42% of employees tend to feel much more successful when informed on company updates or news.

- Three-quarters of employees feel the need to be in the loop concerning their company's business

- 40% of people tend to check LinkedIn every day ("The Deep Disconnect: An HR Data Report", n.d.).

Add LinkedIn Pulse to Your Content Strategy

Pulse is a publishing feature added by LinkedIn to enable a comprehensive audience targeting. While there are a couple of things that are still uncertain about Pulse, there are numerous reasons to make use of it. Some of its advantages are:

- **Increased audience targeting:** Using Pulse, you are able to delve deeper into the demographics of your audience as well as targeting. Pulse enables you to get to the people that will read your content.

- **Get increased social shares**: Top posts ranked by Pulse tend to have about 1843 social shares all in a 48-hour span (York, 2019). Nevertheless, top posts typically are from users that have a larger following. However, there are numerous benefits to landing there.

- **SEO benefits**: there are numerous SEO benefits that Pulse provides like LinkedIn backlinks and content that can be indexed.

- **Content tagging**: You can tag content to increase your traffic once it has been published. What this means is that you are able to create content that can have lasting benefits and searchability, just as a regular blog.

- **Rising competition**: LinkedIn Pulse gets more competitive as the day goes by. There has never been a better time to make use of Pulse.

Some particular contents tend to resonate on LinkedIn Pulse. Some of the top posts included some of the following:

- Articles under a thousand words

- Articles that have great headlines

- Career subject matter content

- Content that does not involve influencers

- Articles with images or visuals

Don't Push Out Stale Content or Go Dark

One of the worst things you can do is leave your LinkedIn page unattended or have it become outdated, as that is likely to cause a lot of damage to your followership. As with almost all social media networks, LinkedIn needs you to continue to engage and remain present. Creating a community on LinkedIn requires you to pay attention and also have monitoring skills. You can stop your page from becoming stale by using the tips below:

- **Frequent Posting**: It is imperative that you post at least once daily, while also aiming to publish a new post each day. You should also attempt to post before work hours and after.

- **Engage**: Comment, reply, and ask questions. You should also join groups on LinkedIn.

- **Always Update**: Cover photos, profiles, business details, and descriptions should be continually updated. New users and content should be added to develop your audience.

- **Add Videos**: It has been shown that 65% more business executives visited a vendor's website after watching a video (York, 2019).

- **Publish Career Opportunities**: Considering there are over 39 million recent grads and students available on LinkedIn, updating your vacancies can help to increase your site's traffic (York, 2019).

- **Humanize Your Page**: Social platform users do not want to join a company that appears to be stiff. Interactions should be genuine and portray a human side to the LinkedIn posts and messages.

Use LinkedIn Analytics to Measure Success

Measuring and tracking the success you attain on LinkedIn is vital to ensuring that your marketing strategy and content deliver results. Below are some LinkedIn metrics which can be used to provide insight on your engagement efforts:

- **Visitor Demographics:** You can find out who reads your content, as well as their job title, industry, location, seniority level, company size, non-employee vs. employee, referral source, and function.

- **Page Views:** How many views your company page received over a particular timespan.

- **Unique Visitors:** How many visitors viewed your page, excluding numerous visits from one user?

- **Impressions:** How many times your post was shown to users on LinkedIn

- **Clicks:** How many clicks your company name, logo, title or content received

- **Followers Acquired:** How many new followers obtained from a sponsored update.

- **Engagements:** Number of impressions divided by interactions

- **Audience:** This shows if a particular post was seen by every one of your followers or a particular group

Achieve More Using LinkedIn

A marketing professional is required to control and communicate using all the LinkedIn connections at their disposal. Nevertheless, this has to be done in a personal and humanistic way to ensure that your posts are viewed. When you make use of the LinkedIn's management tools, you can reach your target audience. It does not matter if your business is just three of you or is an enterprise team numbering 200, you can make use of lots of tools to organize your content that you post on LinkedIn to be a perfect match to your general audience.

Top Mistakes Made on LinkedIn and How to Prevent Them

LinkedIn is the biggest professional social network available, and that is down to the fact that it has more than 610 million users, with over 10 million active job posts ("About LinkedIn", 2019). These figures make it the best professional channel for any industry to create a network on. Nevertheless, LinkedIn is quite a complicated platform to make use of. It is possible to make just a tiny mistake and end up smearing your credibility as a professional, causing you to look unfit and unprofessional for a role. It doesn't matter if you are actively searching for a job or you are not a headhunter.

Not Creating Detailed Goals

One thing headhunters hate seeing when it comes to digital marketers, is them neglecting to create clear goals on LinkedIn for themselves. When you set goals, you can maximize your efforts and ensure that the time you spend on the platform is worthwhile. The ultimate goal is to make connections with like-minded people in the same industry as you, as well as remaining up to date on trends. To do this, however, requires you to invest your effort and time, so you should not expect to see instantaneous results. Instead, see LinkedIn for what it is: a long term strategy that enhances your professional standing. One of your main aims should be showing the value you can provide for any company that hires you. The truth is that recruiters and employers tend to take more interest in what you are able to do for them, rather than what goes on in your personal life. You should position your experience and skills to clearly show your value of businesses, as well as how you can aid them in solving challenging corporate issues.

Not Aligning Your Expertise with Your Profile

The moment headhunters peruse your profile, it is vital that they can gain a clear understanding of the things you do, have done, and what you are able to do for a company. Essentially, it is imperative that your LinkedIn accurately reflects your expertise and career path. When it comes to evaluating an individual's candidacy for a role, LinkedIn can be used as a pertinent data point for employers and digital recruiters alike. You should ensure that your profile does not contain any minor mistakes like misspellings and incorrect grammar, as these are primarily red flags. Typographical errors in your company name, job title or any additional segment of your profile clearly portrays you as either careless or an individual that lacks correct grammar skills, which can be quite a red flag for those that want to attain an executive role. If the aim is to impress whoever it is that stumbles onto your profile, it is essential that you grab their intention as quickly as possible, ensuring that they stay on your profile, your summary and headlines should be compelling and concise to make sure their attention is held. View all your posts as you would a marketing campaign; you are basically selling yourself. You should post content that is relevant solely to your brand, while properly maintaining your profile to make it clear that you have the knowledge and marketing skills or are a proficient professional.

You Have Too Personal a Presence

If you aim to show off a car that you just bought or a video of your pet doing something quickly, then LinkedIn is not the platform for that. It is vital that your profile and the posts it contains are professional and work-centric. Basically, it should not become a private diary where you publicize your individual opinions on subjects that could turn off digital recruiters. Pay close attention to the language and tone you make use of when posting your content and engaging others on the platform. Your complaints and comments should be kept to yourself, particularly when attempting to contribute a professional opinion on a particular topic. LinkedIn is not the platform for you to complain about a client or insult someone else that has a different view from you. Things like this would be seen by recruiters as unwanted aspects or distractions in the workplace, and you are likely to be dropped from the recruiter's potential candidate list.

Not Updating Your LinkedIn

Several marketing professionals tend to abandon their LinkedIn accounts when they are happily employed. The truth is that it is much more seamless to locate a new role when you remain consistently active and update your account. Ensure that you update your account, publish and share content to stay relevant. Nevertheless, it is important not to post too much, as that could have a negative effect.

You should avoid posting self-serving and spammy content. When posting, you should remember that quality is always better than quantity and recruiters are more likely to be impressed with your marketing efforts rather than any personal objectives. You should make sure that your headshot is a professional yet accurate depiction of you. Family holiday pictures and selfies more than 10 years old should be avoided. A profile that has a clear, up-to-date headshot can make a huge difference, as recruiters have a higher probability of clicking on that profile, compared to one without a picture.

Having a LinkedIn profile is something that requires constant attention. It isn't when you are job searching that you start updating or improving it. You should continuously optimize your profile to give it the highest chance of harnessing the opportunities that come your

Ignoring Your Network

It makes no sense to invest all that time and effort into creating your connections and network, only to have it go to waste because you stopped actively engaging and communicating with your network. Remain active by joining industry-relevant groups, as well as engaging with similar interested users. You can improve your professional credibility by engaging with your industry aligned professionals. This also helps you remain updated on innovative developments and trends. This is another scenario where quality is better than quantity. Rather than inviting every individual you meet, you should make connections that are meaningful with individuals in your industry. This helps to enhance your credibility further.

Also, do not immediately begin sending sales pitches as soon as you connect with a person. Investing time to develop authentic relationships is very vital when requesting for favors and pushing sales.

Not Including Keywords

A massive mistake that marketing professionals tend to make while using LinkedIn is not adding keywords to their profiles. You should always remember, at the back of your mind, that LinkedIn is a search engine, which is why it is crucial for you to have keywords in your headline, job description, and professional summary.

For example, if your marketing specialization is automation, you can use keywords such as lead generation and conversion rate. Keywords are identifiers that aid digital recruiters to locate your profile. These keyword essential give your profile a boost.

Not Asking for Help

Sometimes despite your best intentions, it can be possible to overlook some details regarding your profile unintentionally, and digital recruiters understand this. Nevertheless, it is crucial to present your best self on LinkedIn, and that means asking for a second look and general editing at your profile. This could mean asking a peer or a colleague in your chosen industry. It is imperative that you do not dither when asking for help.

LinkedIn is a great place to create your reputation and brand while also establishing important connections in today's busy world. It is crucial that you remain professional; however, you should take advantage of the platform to give a glimpse of your personality. When doing this, you should ensure that you are not too personal, as your aim is to leave a long-lasting impression on recruiters and digital marketing headhunters that stumble upon your profile. The purpose of LinkedIn is to be a place where you can tell your story and show your professional expertise most effectively. You can successfully maximize your opportunities of crafting an outstanding reputation on LinkedIn if you avoid making these mistakes

Chapter 6

Types of Content That Attract

Clients on LinkedIn

One crucial question that should readily come to mind as a social media marketer should be the kind of content that your target audience will like; that is, the sort of content that will not only speak directly to your audience but in the long run expand the visibility of your brand and increase search engine optimization. You've got to bear in mind that each piece of content on social media like LinkedIn or Instagram, has a different and vital role they play concerning your target audience. And so, the kind of content you spread will go a long way to build or mar your brand and help you meet or fall short of marketing metrics.

In this chapter, we're going to be learning the basic tactics you can deploy to get to the heart of your audience by building appropriate and eye-catching content on LinkedIn. The kind of content you capitalize on will regulate how you develop your content strategy and achieve your marketing goals. The following are the types of content you can use to your advantage on the platform.

Blogs

Research shows that more than 80% of social media or conventional marketers who use blog posts, boast a huge return on marketing investment ("2019 Marketing Statistics, Trends & Data — The Ultimate List of Digital Marketing Stats", 2019). Blogs serve as one of the best avenues to upload excellent marketing content. You pay less and spend less time managing them. Blogs help you to reach a large number of audience and engage a variety of social media users. Blogs not only also help share your brand, but it also expands it. With great content, blogs help your brand become the first point of reference by positioning your business as an authority.

LinkedIn gives you the chance to publish blog posts using the LinkedIn publishing platform. These kinds of content come with a lot of invaluable information that will help readers and audience make an informed decision about their business. Blogs come with a lot of entertainment, opinion, expert analysis from industry actors, and practical conversation. Besides, blogs provide the platform for content users to develop internal links on your website. Don't forget, link building is one key thing that promotes your site, especially when targeting SEO. Also bear in mind that to quickly build visibility and effectively boost impressions, blogs are the first and perfect point of contact.

Consider the following types of blog content on LinkedIn:

- Opinion pieces

- Guest blogs & contributor posts

- How-to guides

- Short-form flashes

- Listicles

- Long-form guides

- Newsworthy articles

Images

The importance of images, like blogs, cannot be overemphasized. Images serve as one of the most cost-effective and time-conserving contents that get to the heart of your audience. One important thing is to ensure is that the images you're using have aesthetic value. Don't just post everyday pictures but ones that attract customers and spur new ones to patronize your brand. Images are no doubt, versatile, and sometimes serve the purpose textual content will serve.

Images should not be purposed for the aesthetics of it; they should communicate and tell the story of your brand. Besides posting the images of your products, also ensure you create a storyline and lifestyle that surrounds the product. Ensure you capitalize on powerful keywords behind any image you choose to go with, in the descriptions. Feel free to post thought-provoking images on your LinkedIn page, and you are sure to get tons of engagement.

Types of images to use on LinkedIn:

- Lifestyle (surrounding product/service)

- Events

- Company culture

- Products

- Cartoons

- Memes

- GIFs

Infographics

Are you into business marketing to make a profit and increase client base? Then, never underestimate the power of Infographics. They serve as a prevalent visual for business marketing, giving illustrations that show results of data and research. They help to draw customers and any viewers to your site and blog, because like with images, customers and viewers are drawn to infographics and imagery. They help them to engage in content viewing, liking, and sharing. Infographics serve as excellent methods of earning backlinks. In terms of cost-effectiveness, infographics are rated higher than blogs. Similar to images, you can upload this on your company LinkedIn page with a suitable CTA to reach your audience.

White Papers and Case Studies

A great deal of corporate marketing is done with a detailed summary document of the company. The blockchain and cryptocurrency industry is one industry of global status that has benefited immensely from the use of white paper. Of course, most high-end companies and corporate firms also tap into the innumerable gains of using white papers to sell themselves to their audience and convert many others. A white paper is a simple document that provides a detailed, researched, but concise report about your sector or organization. On the other hand, a case study takes a more in-depth but specific approach. It narrates a particular event or situation that it has helped a client achieve its business or marketing goals. A case study also details the approach and methodology deployed in the process of negotiating, executing, and accessing the project. White papers help you convey and demonstrate the strategic position of your company within the industry as well as showing your company's expertise, innovation, competence, history, and reach.

Hence, when pushing out either of these two long-form documents make sure they convey authoritative, fact-backed, details, and informative information about your company. They should not be fluffed with irrelevance but critical information that readers necessarily have to know about your brand. They must be informative, well-written, and crafted in clear, concise, and industry languages. They must contain a firm's history, industry impact, industry authority, and client loyalty.

They significantly help you grow site/blog impressions. They also connect your brand deeper with your clients while attracting new ones. Both white paper and case studies reports help you generate leads, especially if you make them downloadable and accessible to your email subscribers. Similar to blog content, you can upload them on your LinkedIn page with a CTA directing your audience to perform a specific action of your choice.

Video

Unlike before, video creation has become easier, and its impact on business social media marketing is massive. This is applicable even on LinkedIn as it offers you the capacity to post videos to reach your Audience. You can post videos on your profile, updates, and LinkedIn publisher depending on which suits you best.

With the mobile phone, one can create a quality video that will not only attract customers but also increase search engine optimization. Statistics show that more than 75% of online traffic is driven by online video, with 55% of people reported to be watching videos online daily (Walters, 2015). The tactic is to ensure that you have unique video content that comes with incredible tones, ideas, and engagement. The video content should differentiate your page, blog, or site from others. Interestingly, having just one quality video on your LinkedIn page can drive traffic to your website and increase your conversion by as much as 80% (Lloyd, 2015). Video content should be entertaining, interesting, engaging, and informative. It must address the needs of the customer adequately while also making them have some fun. Bear in mind that video content is an investment, and you wouldn't want to waste your resources on building videos that would not solve any problem or provide useful information to your target audience.

Webinars

Webinars are live events and video conferencing that are specifically serve as a how-to guide. As a live P2P interaction event, webinars allow for participants' intervention and contribution to the conversation. It is a guide session between your brand and your viewers on the platform. The event often utilizes a video, or slideshow along with real-time interpretation. It involves detailed and informative answers and comments from industry and business experts. Participants have the opportunity not only to interact but also make a live chat. It is reported that 20% to 40% of those who attend webinar turn into qualified leads (Nguyen, 2015). You can generate great leads using webinar because it allows you to put a face to your brand and create positive feedback. Take advantage of LinkedIn in promoting your webinar and getting traffic to your website. Lots of people are eager to learn and would be more than willing to check out a webinar that is relevant to them.

Podcasts and Audio

If you're looking at creating consistent interaction with listeners, engage your customers continuously, and build a dedicated following on your LinkedIn page, then podcasts are ideal options. Close to 90% of podcast subscribers have an infectious dedication to the content of the brand they love (Gibbs, 2019). So, if you create a series that has incredible episodes, be sure that you'll be building a following that will increase your visibility and enhance your search engine optimization. The industry is filled with a lot of newsworthy events and information that your customers need to know and be aware of. Try to engage your customers and keep them updated with these events. In that way, you'll be connecting with them most amazingly. You can include links to your podcasts or audio on your LinkedIn profile or attach it to a very appealing image.

Downloadables

Comprehensive contents that you often offer in exchange for emails are what, in technical social media terms, are called 'downloadables'. They include eBooks, checklists, guides, etc. those willing to read your content will only put their email and name to gain access to the content. Sometimes, they will need to create an account with their email and password to be able to access the content. Through that means, you have access to their emails, and you can curate them and subsequently start to send random emails, treating them as 'list of customers.' With downloadables, you're able to generate and build leads while creating a list of potential customers. Add a link to some of your content on your LinkedIn profile or update. A better way is to offer a deal alongside each download. If the downloadable is relevant to your audience, you will undoubtedly draw in massive traffic to your website or get new leads depending on what your objective is.

Types of downloadable:

- eBooks

- Templates

- Checklists

- Reports

- Contents

- Guides

- Courses

Choosing The Right Type of Content

Besides knowing the best kinds of channels through which you can push your content, it is also crucial that you know the best brand for you. Choosing the right type of content for your business depends on five key factors. They are:

- Setting your goal: Ask yourself, 'what key metrics am I aiming to reach with this or that content?

- Stimulate your Audience: Be sure of what types of content your audience responds to.

- Your Platform: Be guided when selecting the platform that your content goes on. Which platform receives the majority of your content? Which one gets the least? Will you redefine the purpose of your post on each?

- Social media: How easy will the content be posted on your social media channels?

- Resources: How much skills, resources, money, and time will be required to be able to do your posting and share your content, given that you will need to create a quality video, image, and other content.

Overall, use a variety of content and never post all-videos, all-images, or all-text. It will become monotonous. Diversify your content to be able to reach a wider audience and increase return on investment.

How to Use Content Marketing Effectively?

Besides its function as a platform for connecting with professionals around the world, LinkedIn is also a productive avenue to get across to your target audience. If you want to reach a more significant number of your target audience, then the growth of your network is essential. The possibility of growing your audience is endless since the platform is sought-after by individuals in search of content relevant to their profession.

Owing to its focus on offering a targeted content approach, most users prefer the LinkedIn platform for content marketing over the use of Twitter. As a result, it has become the heart of business-related content promotion.

Despite its popularity as a content marketing platform, marketers still need to ask themselves a few questions. The main recurring question is if all content gets the same amount of visibility on the platform. In truth, gaining the desired visibility on content is not always a possibility.

Notwithstanding, marketers can reach their target audience rapidly if they remain active on the LinkedIn platform. All they need is an excellent strategy to this effect.

Framework for LinkedIn Content Marketing Planning

Content marketing usually varies depending on the platform you are working on. On most platforms, creating content that your target audience can connect with is the most crucial factor. On the LinkedIn platform, things are a bit different. In this case, gaining the attention of stakeholders in an industry is the primary purpose of the content you create.

It has become apparent that LinkedIn is one of the best platforms that offers results that are relevant to your business goals. These results include the gain of trustworthy leads and engagement with heavyweights in a particular industry. Content marketing on LinkedIn may seem to progress at a slow pace, but business owners are finding meaning in being patient.

Unlike with other social media platforms, the operations and mechanics of LinkedIn differs. LinkedIn users depend on endorsements from reliable individuals. These endorsements are similar to the likes and shares that show the presence of a profile on other social platforms. Other users on the LinkedIn platform understand an endorsement to indicate consent towards a profile.

To differentiate LinkedIn from other social media platforms, some statistics have been shared by brands. These statistics focus on the effect of some of the crucial indexes about the results of a business. To ensure you can keep up with the difference in the LinkedIn dynamics, a content marketing strategy that is independent and organic is necessary for companies, both B2C and B2B.

When engaging in LinkedIn content marketing, there are numerous content marketing tools and strategies available to implement. These help in creating a proper strategy on the platform. The showcase and company pages are features that promote the creation of service leadership while InMail and other similar features enable companies to engage in production and brand awareness activities.

When a brand sets a goal to boost their authority, the promotion of webinars, eBooks, and events is vital. For the best form of advertisement, the sponsored posts feature on the platform is suitable.

Any brand that intends to connect with a target audience that is relevant to their operations must implement these features. These are some easy ways to make the most out of the content marketing on LinkedIn. The results of these actions are beyond satisfactory.

To achieve these results, there are various steps an organization can follow. Here are some of the steps that can help ease the process:

Work Towards Your Network Growth

From previous discussions and comparisons, you should understand LinkedIn is unique. This makes it different from other social platforms. Therefore, the approach you take on LinkedIn must also differ.

In its purest form, promoting network growth involves sending invitations to other users with similar interests. Additionally, there are other simple steps you can take to achieve this objective. You should provide a fully detailed profile page, become an active member of different groups, connect with others by creating personalized messages to send, and ensure your LinkedIn URL has your email signature attached.

There has been a massive boost in the number of LinkedIn users since Microsoft purchased the company. According to the LinkedIn website, there are currently over 610 million users on the platform ("About LinkedIn", 2019).

With this number of users, you can build a broader network that will get more users to notice the content you publish on the platform quickly.

Company Page Set Up

You have gone through an in-depth explanation on how to set up the company page in an earlier chapter. If you are one of the users that is still without a company page, you should go back and follow the instructions. If you want to solidify the place of your organization as an authority, then creating a company page is the first step you must take.

The details of your company's identity, nature, and business operations are some of the critical information that the company page must provide to visitors. For proper branding purposes and to get individuals to associate an image to your business, uploading a logo is crucial.

Although it provides information on the company, the page is also the center of the content distribution strategy of the organization. Both in the LinkedIn search and on various search engines, the page is essential for enhancing the visibility of your brand.

Getting news across to your followers becomes more straightforward with the company page. The strategy you come up with must include a plan that defines how you upload weekly updates. Topics you can cover include:

- Industry trends

- Advice that is business related

- Newsfeed of the company

Followers will only remain interested if the updates are consistent.

Goal Driven Content Marketing

There must be a goal behind your content strategy if you want to get across to the target audience. Some of the vital objectives your strategy must accomplish include:

- Provision of authentic information – Authenticity depends on your ability to look beyond making sales. Information on the page should also be helpful and useful to the readers. This information can be in the form of ideas, industry updates, and unique knowledge

- An approach that interests readers – If the content is boring, no one will get to read it. Make it more fun and enjoyable to read by including graphics to your content

- Don't focus on your page/group alone – It will be challenging to connect with new users if your sole focus is on your page. Get other groups/pages to work to your advantage by posting relevant comments on their posts. These groups are your peers on the platform and engaging with their content will get them to notice yours

- Be engaging – Any content you post on your page must be curated to promote engagement. If your content can get readers to comment and discuss, then it will do an excellent job in getting others to visit your page

Design and Implement a Plan that is Specific to the Newsfeed

The plan for your newsfeed should involve providing vital information regarding your company and the industry. Here are some tips on the information to upload:

If your research shows a large number of job seekers on the market, then you can assist by sending invites for walk-in interviews at your company or offer job tips

- You can also choose to provide relevant information concerning relevant job opportunities

- Create an action plan to tell these job seekers about skills they can learn and develop to improve their chances

- Inform them about the prospects of your company and what professionals can gain

- Providing a link to a video or website of your company is also a good idea

Having a clear picture of content that will be relevant to the current market will help in developing a great strategy. This is how you move in a positive direction.

Be Selective with the Groups You Join

Joining a group doesn't have to be about taking the first choice that comes your way. Any group you join should be one that is relevant to the niche of your business operations. This should be your goal.

Notwithstanding the niche of your business, there are usually several groups available to join. This allows you to connect and interact with competitors and peers in the industry.

There are different ways of joining a group can offer benefits. It can help enhance the visibility of your company and boost traffic to your page. If you want to receive information that is relevant to your growth, you must also develop the habit of sharing ideas and information you have.

Identifying the right group is easy if you know what to look out for. First, you should find a group with a decent number of members. You should also check the level of interaction among members of the group. There is a statistics box that offers the information you need regarding a group.

To get an idea of the level of interaction, locate the number of posts in the last month. This should include both the number of articles and the number of comments on each article.

Avoid Thoughts or Messages that are Personal

If you want to connect with professionals on the LinkedIn platform, then you must also be a professional. Your professionalism must be identifiable in the articles you post, your comments, and interactions with other users.

To avoid anything that would seem unprofessional, personal thoughts and messages must be considered crossing the line on this platform. Despite your good intentions, you must not use the LinkedIn platform in the same manner as other social platforms.

If you are expecting other users to send you congratulatory remarks on the acquisition of a new house, you may find yourself blocked from the connections list of most users.

Be Patient

Content marketing on LinkedIn doesn't provide immediate results. Understanding this simple truth is the only way you can make progress on this platform. There will be times when the responses you get is far below your projections.

The trick is to remain active on the platform. At this point, visit the pages of your competitors and post relevant comments. It is usually slow, but, you will notice that you are steadily improving your visibility on the platform.

Actual responses may also fall short of your projections due to differences in time zones of users.

Have a Schedule for Your Updates

Understanding that LinkedIn is not the same as other social media platforms will save you a lot of stress. You must keep repeating this phrase to yourself. Be careful in your approach to posting updates.

Promoting your business on Facebook or Twitter, sharing and uploading the same post over and over may get you the responses you desire. This is why a lot of users post several updates in a day. On LinkedIn, you won't like the results of these actions.

You may receive the label of a spammer if you keep up these actions on LinkedIn. Instead, be smart about your posts and limit them to a maximum of two updates in a day. These updates must be relevant to the interests of the industry but also try to offer different perspectives in each update.

The Shorter, the Better

Do you want more readers on your posts? Then learn to give them what they want. In addition to finding relevant content, readers also want content that is straight to the point. To boost the readability of your content, learn to use bullet points.

To further simplify the read, your subheadings should be self-explanatory. Remember, nobody wants to spend time reading your stories.

Create Attention-Grabbing Headlines

If you want to get your content across to your audience and also ensure they read it, then the headline you use must be accurate and intriguing to the reader.

Consistency is Key

Consistency is merely creating a pattern and ensuring you stick to it. In this case, the pattern you develop concerns your updates. Your updates should be regular and consistent. Posting a large number of updates in one day and disappearing for the next month is a recipe for disaster.

Instead, spread these updates to make sure you have something new to post every day.

Make the Most of the Publish Platform

There are numerous benefits to using the LinkedIn Publish Platform. You receive the rights for any article you publish, and it remains your work. There is also the possibility of LinkedIn annotating the work, sharing it, or selling advert space on the content page.

As long as you write an article that offers value and is relevant, you can reach your target audience with ease.

Integrate the Use of SlideShare

Sometimes, the outcome of your eBooks or blogs may not be what you desire. To solve this problem with ease, LinkedIn offers the use of SlideShare as a solution. It is a solution that simplifies the process of adding visual content to your content marketing strategy.

To make use of SlideShare, the first step is to create a company page on this platform. You can then link the SlideShare page of the company to the LinkedIn page of the company. Once connected, any content or presentation you create on SlideShare will appear on LinkedIn.

Since a lot of users interact more with visual content, an excellent SlideShare presentation can grow your followers by boosting engagement. Simply pick a topic of interest or one that is currently trending and use images to simplify it as much as you can. It is essential you assess readability.

Don't miss out on the opportunity to reap massive rewards by implementing a content strategy that is effective on the LinkedIn platform. It is a simple way to outdo the competition.

Chapter 7

How to Increase Your Connections

The core focus of LinkedIn is to make connections, ranging from people you already know to those you aspire to know. Now the platform tops half a billion users spread around over 200 countries ("About LinkedIn", 2019), which makes it a top option among social media platforms, for connecting with potential hires, business partners, and B2B prospects.

Although this platform is a clear leader in comparison to other social media platforms when it has to do with networking with professionals, many users still find it very intimidating to use this platform. And for many new users, including marketers, the major problem they deal with is how to increase their connections. Many of them wonder who they should connect with and who they should not connect with. Ultimately, pondering on these questions can make it quite slow to increase connections on the platform.

Even though the platform has half a billion users, it can be tedious to find 500 followers or more to get the status of a superuser and make more sales. The reason is that after you have used up your contact list, it can be challenging to find others to connect with, particularly when you want to ensure the connections are relevant and would be of value to your network down the road. As a marketer, you want to add people who can convert to buyers later on or people who will provide you with opportunities down the road.

That being said, this chapter will cover some helpful techniques for increasing your connections. But first, let's explore the degrees of connections in LinkedIn.

Various Degrees of Connection

The individuals on your LinkedIn are known as connections. Your network consists of your 1st-degree, 2nd-degree, and 3rd-degree connections, alongside individuals in the same groups as you. To build your network, you need to send an invitation to connect with other members of the platform along with your email contact. Another way is to accept invites from other individuals. The way you can communicate with a person on the platform is dependent on the degree of connection you have with them.

Below is a breakdown of all the degrees:

- 1st-degree connections: These are individuals who you are connected to directly, either because they accepted your invitation to connect or vice versa. You will spot the 1st-degree sign beside their name, on their profile, or in search results. You can reach out to these individuals by sending them a message via the platform.

- 2nd-degree connections: These consists of individuals who share a connection with your 1st-degree connections. You will spot the icon for 2nd degree beside their name on their profile and in search results. To invite them to connect, you need to hit the connect button which you can spot on their profile page. You can also contact them via an InMail.

- 3rd-degree connections: These individuals are connected to the 2nd-degree connections you have. As before, you can see the icon for 3rd degree beside their names on their profiles and in search results.

Connecting with these individuals is a bit different from the others.

1. If their full names are on display, you will be able to send an invitation by hitting Connect.

2. If you can only see the first letter of their last name, you will be unable to hit Connect. However, you can reach out to them using InMails.

- Members in the same group as you: These consist of people in your network because you are a part of the same group. The member profile consists of a Highlight page which shows the groups you are both members of. To reach out to them, you can do it straight from the group or send them a message on LinkedIn.

Now that you understand the various degrees of connections, let's have a look at why having an extensive network is vital.

Why Is a Large Network Significant?

Having a more extensive network may not be as personal as having smaller networks, but this does not mean they are not vital. LinkedIn offers a 30,000 max number of connections, which you don't need to attain to be privy to all the benefits of a vast network. However, your goal should be for 500+ to capitalize on your profile "completeness" from the perspective of LinkedIn

Below are a few reasons why you may want to channel more energy into expanding your network:

- Enhance your LinkedIn search results: Except if a recruiter is leveraging on the pricey LinkedIn Recruiter or using the full name of a person to run a search, LinkedIn search results will consist of only individuals connected to the person running the search as first, second or third-degree connections on the platform.

- The higher your number of connections, the higher the possibility that you will show up in the search results of users, even if these users are a third-degree connection. LinkedIn does not sort users using the degree of connection, which makes it possible for a third-degree connection to be at the top of your search results. Ultimately, if you don't have a reasonable number of connections on LinkedIn, your visibility is severely restricted.

- Your Published Content will get more reach: The instant you become an elite on LinkedIn, any content you publish has a higher level of popularity in comparison to those who have smaller networks. The reason behind this is simple. The blogging platform of LinkedIn informs users when a connection has published a post. What this means for you with a more significant number of connections is that more users will be informed when you publish any new content. The outcome is a load of engagement with your content, which is every marketer's desire. The enhanced engagement you get also means you have a higher possibility of your content being featured in LinkedIn Pulse, and once this happens, you are sure of even higher engagement.

- More views to your profile: There is a high possibility that when you add someone new to your connection, they will end up taking a look at your profile. And if your profile is buyer-focused, a reasonable amount of these users who check out your profile could convert to sales. Now, the instant you begin to add and accept more connections on LinkedIn, the more profile views you get, which means higher chances of conversion. Some people get as much as a thousand profile views each week. Imagine the possible ROI this could bring you!

- More Endorsements: The higher the number of your connections, the more endorsements you will get. Endorsements are similar to badges of honor, which offer you more credibility. When you don't that many connections, you have a reduced amount of individuals in your network endorsing you. When you get a streak of endorsements on your profile, it can make it look fantastic and credible to potential buyers. However, this may be close to impossible to attain if your network is not vast.

Now that you understand why growing your network is vital to you as a marketer or individual, let's have a look at some categories of people you can connect with to grow your network.

People to Connect With

The following are some of the people you can connect with to enhance your network:

Professionals You Know

These are people you have worked with or still work with. You can run into them in events and have a conversation there. These individuals are part of your physical professional life, so you want to make them part of a professional life online too. They know what you do, and they are the ones you contact when you require someone skilled in a specific field. These are the individuals that will endorse you and vice versa.

Professionals You Don't Know Yet but Desire to Meet

You may have never had a physical meeting with them, but you came across their profile, and you saw something they have achieved that you would want for yourself. Perhaps you have heard them speak at a conference at some point, and you desire to do the same. Their fantastic wealth of experience is all you ever wanted for yourself. These individuals could end up being your mentors, colleagues, or employers later down the road, but checking out their profile frequently gives you the drive to go on for a while. You need to add these individuals to your connections.

People from Your Background Which Include Family and Friends

When you first think about your seatmate in high school, which you have not come in contact with for a long time, and is now in a sector opposite to yours, you may believe he/she is not relevant to you. Well, this is far from the truth because aside from the fact that individuals from a diverse range of sectors offer you a point of view different from yours which can also be quite beneficial in the long run as people tend to know other people. You can never tell who may be of help to you later in the future and vice versa.

Individuals with Numerous Connections

For these individuals, it may be the work they do or just how they are. But some people have a considerable amount of contacts, and they belong in this category. Those who get numerous contacts can act as the missing link between you and other people you need to meet, or jobs you so desire. Also, these individuals may not be difficult to contact and connect with, since they most likely add all individuals.

Individuals with Prospects

These individuals consist of those who probably just kicked off an idea and ran a little business or something minor. However, even if they do not seem like they would be of any benefit to you presently, you never can tell what they will achieve later on. Since this is a platform for networking, why not give them a chance? Connect with them and see how it goes; you never can say what the future holds.

Individuals with Unique Skills

Do you know someone who is uniquely skilled with something? Maybe he/she knows how to break a computer apart and put it back together, or perhaps they are just experts in specific subjects. These individuals can get you out of the most complex situations without any hassle. He/she knows how to save the day. Add this person, because you will most likely need his/her help numerous times in the future.

Your Most Awful Critic

This could include that boss you worked with before, or a lecturer in school, who made you do a ton of hard work before you were able to achieve a goal. This is someone who will never shower you with praise if he/she believes that you did not put in your best to achieve a particular task. What this person says to you may hurt, but if you want to get to the top quickly, nothing helps any faster than a little constructive criticism. Follow this set of individuals and embrace what they have to offer you.

Now that you understand some vital people to connect with let's check out a few techniques you can use in increasing your connections.

Tailor Your Connection Requests

Go through the suggested connections offered by LinkedIn frequently. Make it your objective to locate individuals in the same niche or industry as you and connect with them. Make efforts to connect with four or more people at a go. However, when you want to connect with that person, don't just hit the connect button, as doing so may send a generic request to the person. As opposed to this, head to the profile page of the individual you want to connect with and hit the connect button you find there. Using this method will show up a box which will give you the chance to include a personal note alongside your connection request. From here, try to tailor it in a way that is unique to that person. To do this, consider the following:

- How did you know the individual?

- Where or how did you meet?

- What is your reason for connecting?

For instance, if the person you want to connect with works in a similar niche to yours, attach a note like this: *"I have noticed some of your posts, and love your point of view. I would love to connect."*

Creating personalized connection requests does not take more than a minute or two, but if done well, the possibility of people responding to your request positively will be much higher —and you will have a better opportunity of getting a sale.

Reach Out to Those You Meet Physically

The traditional method of meeting people physically is not going to fade anytime soon. It is still a significant aspect of networking. LinkedIn was developed to connect with people you must have networked with at some point. You network with a specific person in the business, locate their profile, run a search for their attributes and skills and add them to your contact with the hopes that they could aid in boosting your career in some way. This is why the platform is as popular as it is today. If you want to increase your connections, it would be ideal to network a little in the real world. Take part in events and other professional meetings. Introduce yourself to new people, even when you go to the grocery.

Did you meet someone at an event or a conference? Perhaps you both volunteer for the same charity? How about the owner of the store you get your groceries? These are all great avenues to create new connections and grow your network. It is easy to let go of those we meet in the real world, but if you can run a quick search on the platform, you are most likely going to find out they have an account and will be more than willing to approve your connection request.

Put Goals in Place

It is less difficult to achieve something when you have a goal in mind. Giving yourself a target of getting 50 or more connections each week may seem impossible, but that is not the case, mainly if you spread that number to each day. For instance, instead of the goal of getting 50 connections at once, try setting a goal of 10 connections each day of the week.

Don't forget that when setting up goals, you need to ensure that they are realistic. Also, you need to remember to be careful about this, as there are guidelines to appropriate LinkedIn behavior you need to follow. You don't want to spam those that won't be of value to what you do. If your goal is to get clients that convert, quality is still more vital than quantity. Also, you need to remember that not all your requests to connect will be approved. Don't feel bad about this as it is perfectly normal. Some individuals won't approve connection requests from people they have not met before. If this happens, don't dwell on it, move further into achieving your goal and chances are, later down the road, when you have a reasonable number of connections, and they feel you can offer them value now, they will be sending the request instead

Post Status Updates Each Day

Being active on LinkedIn is vital, and an easy way to begin this is to post status updates each day. You should consider your updates the same as you would any post you make on social media. However, you need to ensure it adds actual value. Speak about what you do and add a CTA.

When you remain in your connections feeds continuously, it offers them more chances to leave comments, share, and like your posts. With this interaction, you get on the radar of their connections, too, which offers you one more method of growing your network. When there are lots of individuals engaging with content you post, it serves as additional credibility that you are a professional in your field.

Incorporate the URL to your LinkedIn profile in your Email Signature

Your LinkedIn profile functions in a range of ways, all of which are to your benefit. It acts as a testimonial, resume, project portfolio, social proof and evidence that you are skilled in your field all in a single platform, In your email signature, instead of directing potential clients to your account on Facebook, you can redirect them to your profile on LinkedIn instead.

Doing this is straightforward too. The first step is to copy your LinkedIn vanity URL, which is a clickable link, that is easy to remember and point out. Head to the info page on your profile and hit the gear icon beside your LinkedIn URL. Then, when the next page comes up, search for your Public Profile URL page, where you can make modifications. The instant you have your vanity URL, incorporate it to your email signature so it will be easier for individuals to connect with you. Remember to include your business card too while doing this.

Join groups

Invest some of your time each month to look for new and relevant LinkedIn group to join. Then, when you do, ensure you engage with all the groups you join as frequently as you can, liking comments of other people and leaving comments.

Groups are great for doing market research, engaging with those on your niche and those that are not, as well as posting links to your updates to get more views. When users come across you in groups and communicate with you for a while, they will have a higher possibility of sending a request to connect. Better still, you may come across a business partner or new customer via a group.

To locate groups, you can become a member of, run a search for groups on the LinkedIn search box using relevant keywords. The instant you have located a group and joined, contribute by beginning a conversation or asking a question. Remember to join small groups as well as large ones.

To take it further, you can create a group of your own. This will offer you immediate credibility because people love to network with those who are experts in their fields with a lot of connections. When anyone joins a group you created, they will have a higher possibility of connecting with you, as the owner of the group. This is because they know you already and like the things you share.

Integrate Keywords in Your profile

To ensure people don't have issues finding you, incorporate keywords in your profile, as we covered earlier. There are three sections you will want to pay attention to which are your headline, experience, and summary sections. These sections are searchable, which is why integrating keywords will ensure you are more searchable, boosting the possibility to create new connections. You need to be creative when filling out these sections, maximize your characters allowed, and use relevant keywords in your niche people are likely to search for.

Post relevant content on LinkedIn's Publishing Platform

LinkedIn offers a publishing platform which ensures anyone can post appealing posts with ease, seem like a professional in his/her field, and demonstrate his/her knowledge.

Three of your posts are showcased above your profile. One major significance of this platform is that any content you upload can be seen by the entire users of the platform and not just those you are connected to. This can help in enhancing your exposure. When a wider audience notices you, it will aid you in developing your network by getting to all the layers available on the platform. Individuals who won't typically come across your profile in search results will be able to learn what services you render and how you can assist them in solving their problems. Ensure you publish content frequently and also strive to make sure your content is current and fresh. If you are not sure about what to publish, you can repurpose past blogs or content you have written.

Take advantage of Images

When you capitalize on images for making social posts, it can tremendously enhance your engagement with individuals in your network and open you up to prospective connections. According to research, utilizing visual content can aid in enhancing views by as much as 11 times. Try to shake things up a bit. Instead of sharing just links, make efforts to include photos too.

Engage with The Connections You Presently Have

Check out your feed frequently and comment on, like, and share the content posted by your connections. When you get a new connection, you can trigger relationships by leaving comments on their updates. Also, you can develop an audience by partaking in conversations on popular posts in your field. By interacting this way, you will be more visible to a more significant number of people. Better still, some of these individuals may be interested in knowing you better, which translates to new connections.

Use Other Social Platforms in Promoting Your LinkedIn URL

If you are leveraging other social media channels, there is usually a section to add a bio. Taking full advantage of this provided section could be a fantastic way to drive loads of connection to your LinkedIn, especially when you urge viewers to do so and if you have a reasonable following on that specific platform.

Also, you can go further in promoting your LinkedIn profile on this platform by posting the link in a tweet, photo, video, status update, among others. It is a fantastic way to use your presence on other social channels to the fullest. Just ensure you remember to claim your vanity URL to be able to get this done.

Use your Email Contacts

At some point, you may have gotten an email from LinkedIn with something in the lines of: *"Jack would like to connect with you on LinkedIn"* and then you begin to wonder who Jack is and why he would want to connect with you? This is what importing your email contacts on the LinkedIn platform can do. It brings in all your contacts, so they each get a connection request.

This may be annoying depending on how you look at it, but it does not mean this is not a great way to grow your connections. Include as many emails as you can, ranging from your email, work email, university email, or side business email. The reason is that on all of these emails, you may have a massive amount of contacts that you may have sent an email at one point in time. All of these individuals, even if they are not on the platform, will be sent an email from you requesting that they "Connect" with you on the LinkedIn platform.

Besides, if you are worried about sending a LinkedIn request to specific people whom you would rather not, you have the capacity to screen the list of people that will be sent your "Connect with me on LinkedIn" email.

Send Connect Requests to LIONS

LION connotes "LinkedIn Open Networkers." They are a group of professionals on the LinkedIn platform that do not mind random individuals who they don't know, connecting with them. In essence, these are individuals that will certainly approve your connection request.

However, LIONS may differ in quality, but this is not a problem. Feel free to connect to any of them. The reason for this is: if you build your first connections, regardless of who they are, you will be provided access to their second connections. Ultimately, if the LION you connect to is not relevant to you in any way, the individuals who are connected to the LION, who you are not connected to, may be of relevance to you.

Locating LIONS is also very easy, as these individuals place it on their profile. You can run a search via the LinkedIn search bar by inputting keywords like "L.I.O.N," "LIONS," and a range of others to begin connecting with these individuals. Additionally, you can include LION in your profile as well, so that those who are in search of open networkers can locate you and add you too, leading to an increase in your connections.

Include Individuals Who Check Out Your Profile

LinkedIn offers you access to a page which lets you see those who viewed your profile. You can go through this page to view a list of users on LinkedIn that paid a visit to your profile of recent and read your information.

Now, these people may have looked through your profile for some reason. Either because they came across you via a keyword search, had an interest in you or a content you posted which led them to you. Perhaps, your profile was made visible by LinkedIn under their 'People You Should Follow' tab. Notwithstanding the reason, these individuals have shown some level of interest in you, and that is all you need to connect with them. If you send a connection request to all of those that checked out your profile, you are likely going to be accepted by most of them.

Also, doing the opposite of this has the same effect. If you check out the profile of other individuals, they will find you in their 'Who's Viewed Your Profile' page. If the number of profiles you view is substantial, at least a little amount of these people will request to connect with you.

Publish Videos

The LinkedIn video feature is one which is still a little new, and for this reason, the algorithm gives priority to video content. Also, because the competition is not so much when it comes to videos, you have a higher possibility to leave a lasting impact with videos. The video feature has provided lots of marketers with fantastic results, so it's certainly something you need to exploit.

For every kind of brand and individual, LinkedIn can offer you a range of benefits. An effortless way of taking advantage of what this platform has to provide you is to increase your number of LinkedIn connections. There is no better time to exploit it than now.

Chapter 8

Steps in Creating Ads on LinkedIn

LinkedIn is an excellent tool for networking with professionals of like minds. However, what many marketers do not know is that LinkedIn offers a very commanding ads platform. If you are already utilizing other platforms like Facebook or Instagram, then you may want to take advantage of LinkedIn as well.

In this chapter, we will be taking a look at how to set up your first ad campaign on LinkedIn. With that in mind, let's move on to how ads work on this platform.

How do LinkedIn Ad Campaigns Function?

Ads on LinkedIn is a process consisting of two-steps. The first step includes developing your campaign, and the next has to do with the creation of the ad. We will delve into the steps in order.

Developing Your Campaign

Your LinkedIn ad campaigns will not be on the same platform as the typical LinkedIn you use for connecting with other professionals. Instead, it is on a platform known as the LinkedIn Marketing Solutions platform. You need to head to that page, to begin with, your campaign. After successfully opening the page, you need to pick: "Create Ad."

Next, if you have not done so, a prompt will come up requesting you make a LinkedIn Campaign Manager account. Here, you need to include the LinkedIn page of your company if there is one available. Next, you will be redirected to your member dashboard where you need to include your billing data if you have not done so. This is a necessary step to unlock the account.

Via the Campaign Manager or your dashboard, a Create Campaign button will be visible. Select this, and you will be greeted with a page to begin developing your campaign.

Now, when it comes to developing your campaign, the first step is to pick a Campaign Group and give your campaign a name. The role of the Campaign Group is to aid you in organizing your campaign. You can choose to make a new Group or use the default group.

The instant you have selected the Campaign group and giving it a name, you can now move on to selecting your campaign objective.

Select your objective

Your objective is the action you want individuals to take when they view your ads. LinkedIn offers you three themes for campaigns. They include:

- Considerations

- Awareness

- Conversion

There are numerous campaigns objectives to pick from under these themes. They are:

- Website visits: If your goal is to push traffic to your landing pages and website, this is the objective to go with. As stated by LinkedIn, this is also the campaign to use if you want to enhance the awareness of your brand.

- Video views: This will help enhance your video exposure to those who have a high possibility of engaging with them.

- Engagement: if your goal is to enhance your LinkedIn Company Page followers and enhance your content engagement, this is the goal to choose.

- Lead Generation: This will display a form for a lead generation already filled profile information LinkedIn users who have a high possibility of engaging with the form.

Once you have determined what your objective is, you can now move on to choosing your target audience.

Pick Your Target Audience

The next step is to determine your target audience parameters. When you target individuals who view your ad, it can aid in achieving its campaign objective. The more relevant and specific an ad is to your viewers, the better its performance. LinkedIn gives you the capacity to target your audience using various categories, which we will elaborate on below.

It is not essential for you to utilize every option available; however, the more precise your targeting criteria is, the more the audience you pick is likely to find it relevant. This means you have more possibility of getting a better return on investment. You will first be required to answer a few questions; like the language you want your ads to show up in. LinkedIn supports 20 languages, including French, Spanish, and German, which means you have loads of options depending on your audience.

You will also need to pick no less than one location for your ad. Depending on what your business is; it may be of help to be more specific here. You may want to exempt any locations close to your campaign location, so you don't use up your budgets on locations where your ad is not of value.

Now, select "+ Add new targeting criteria."

The following are a few targeting criteria you can pick from:

- Company: If the audience you want to target has a specific employer, you will be able to target it directly, even using its name. It is not essential for you to use specific names, but LinkedIn gives you the chance to target organizations using the sector like Finance, Health, and the size of the company.

- Interests: A terrific perk LinkedIn offers is the capacity to become a member of groups consisting of professionals with like minds, where you can speak about topics and trends in the industry. If your audience has a lot of interest in a specific topic, this may be a great kind of targeting for you.

- Demographics: If your audience is heavily focused on a specific age group or gender, you may want to use this option to determine them.

- Job Experience: If the service or product you are offering is ideal for CIOs, targeting individuals who have the title "CIO" will enhance your conversions and save you cash in the long run. You can also pick precise job titles or pick from years of experience, seniority, and job functions. From the CEO of health organizations to associates at law firms, you have the chance of targeting specific categories of individuals for your ads. The audience you are targeting may also possess a specific set of skills, ranging from financial planning, business management, or marketing. Consider what your target audience is skilled at and aspects they strive to succeed. Then, with your ad, target individuals who have similar skills.

- Education: If you plan on targeting individuals with a specific background in education, you have the chance to target your ads using schools. For instance, if you need to target the alumni association of a specific school, you can use a LinkedIn ad. Also, you can modify your targeting using degree or field of study.

The instant you have determined the targeting criteria for your ad, you can store it as a template for use in your future campaigns. You also can enable LinkedIn to spread your audience to consist of individuals who share similarities with your target audience. After you have chosen your target audience, the next step is to determine your ad format.

Determine your Ad Format

The next step is to pick the format for your ad. There are various kinds of LinkedIn ads you can choose from, which include:

- Text ads: These are small ads that are displayed at the top of the LinkedIn page. They consist of text only and may also show up beneath the people you may know section. These ads are straightforward to create, and you can use a cost per thousand impressions or cost per click model to set up. Depending on the kind of texts you use, it can break or make your ad conversions.

- Single image ads: These have a single image and are displayed on the newsfeed on organic content.

- Job ads: Advertise available jobs and utilize the profile data of the user to personalize every ad. They can only be seen on the desktop platform of LinkedIn.

- Carousel ads: These consist of two images or more and are displayed on the newsfeed.

- Message ads/Sponsored InMail: These are sent to the LinkedIn inbox of your target audience. These messages include a CTA button, body text, custom greeting, and the capacity to include a link to the body of the message. You can purchase these messages on a cost per send basis. This implies that you will make payment for every unit of message delivered.

- Follower ads: Promotes the LinkedIn page of the company and uses the data from profile to personalize each ad. However, these ads can only be seen by users on the desktop platform of LinkedIn.

When you go through the various kinds of ads, you will observe that the 'projected results box', which you can find at the right, changes. This feature helps in analyzing the parameters of your campaign like the targeting, budget, bid, etc. It also considers advertisers and campaigns similar to yours.

Monitor this box while determining the type of ad to go with. As a starter, picking a specific kind of ad may be dependent on your budget. Determine what is important to you, then you can determine the ad that is suitable for your needs.

Placement

The next thing to do is to determine if you desire that your ad be exhibited on the LinkedIn Audience Network, which offers more exposure and reach to your campaign, among LinkedIn's third-party sites and platforms. However, you are only privy to this option depending on the kind of ad you use.

Also, you can decide to block or remove specific applications, categories, and websites in the Network if you want.

Determine your Budget & Schedule

Next, implement the budget, bidding, and scheduling options that are ideal for your needs.

Budget

Place a daily budget for what is within your spending limit. Before you invest a lot of cash into a single campaign, you need to test and measure how successful each ad variation and campaign are. You don't want to channel all your resources into an ad that your target audience does not find relevant.

Let's assume you are the Chief Marketer at an established confectionary. You can presume that the majority of your target market consists of brides, and for this reason, you channel all your campaigns to bridal groups. However, after investing a lot of cash into it, the leads you got was less than what you anticipated. Then you made additional research which proved that this was not the right move, and you later found out that there were lots of people close to your store on LinkedIn, looking for cakes for birthday parties and corporate events. Won't it have been great to know this in advance before you invested a considerable chunk of your budget on Ads?

LinkedIn gives you the capacity to target a niche market; however, it's still best to do your research first. If you do so and find out a campaign is doing well, then you can channel a more significant amount of funds towards it.

Schedule

Pick a start date for your campaign. You can signify that your campaign is continuously displayed or ends at a specific time.

Bid Type

Here, you have three choices to pick from which include:

- Automated bid: gives LinkedIn the authority to decide the amount that will bring out the most of your campaign objective and any option you choose to go with, be it Impressions, Clicks, or Conversions.

- Maximum (CPM) pay-per-1,000 Impressions bid: Here, any time your ad is seen by 1,000 individuals on the platform, you will be charged a specific amount. However, if you are using the LinkedIn Audience Network option, this will not be available to you.

- Maximum (CPC) or cost-per-click bid: here, every time an individual clicks on your ad, you will be charged. A bid range is suggested by LinkedIn based on your ad competition and your budget. The higher the number of advertisers bidding on a campaign similar to yours, the more your bid has to be. This bid is the max your charge will be. If the present rate is less than your peak bid, you will only need to pay only for the current bid.

It can be a little complicated to choose the idea max bid. When deciding if to go with CPM or CPC, your end goal should be your major consideration.

Is your plan to ensure as many individuals as possible view your ads? Or to assist them with a branding campaign or something similar? If the latter is the case, going with a CPM may be an ideal choice.

On the other hand, if your goal is to ensure a higher amount of individuals click on your ads to generate new leads, or push more traffic to your site, then going with CPC may be an excellent choice.

When it comes to determining your ideal bid, you may have to experiment a little. LinkedIn will offer you a suggested bid, which can be a great place to begin. Then, consider the period your audience is more active online. This is the period you will want to make higher bids so you can be confident that your ads will be the ones viewed. Also, ensure LinkedIn is the ideal location to reach your audience. Various users use various kinds of social media platforms. Experiment with your bids and see what works and what does not.

Conversion Tracking

Finally, you have the choice of putting conversion tracking in place for your campaign. This will aid you in monitoring and measuring what people do after they click on your ads.

Conversion tracking is not mandatory when it has to do with putting your campaign in place; however, it can offer your business colossal value.

To implement conversion tracking, hit "+ Add conversions." When you do, a new window will show up, where you will give your conversion a name, then you pick your ideal conversion settings and determine how you want to track your conversions.

Now, you have set up your ad campaign, but that is not all. When you want to go further, remember to save. Note that the instant you do, you will be unable to change your ad format and objective, so you have to be sure that this is what you want before you go any further.

Setting Up Your Ad(s)

After establishing your core ad considerations, you will get a prompt asking you to begin developing it and deciding the way LinkedIn will showcase and alternate your ad variations if you choose to create more than one.

To begin, select "Create new ad." When you do, a new screen will show up, where you will develop an ad copy, associate it with a specific image, and go through the various arrangement options.

There are a few things to note here which include:

- Ad image: This is the graphic or artwork that will be seen by your audience for your ad. It has to be uploaded as a .png or .jpg file which is 2MB or less. Also, it has to be 100x100 pixels.

- Ad headline: This is the core message that will be seen by your audience. You will be unable to exceed 25 characters here.

- Ad description: This what your ad contains, which can be as long as 75 characters. It needs to be relevant to the individual looking at the ad, and the page you are directing them, or the offer in place.

- Destination URL: This is the location your audience will be directed to anytime they click on your ad. Check once more to ensure the URL is correct.

The instant you are through including all of this data, you can see the changes in the Preview box. The moment you select "Create," you will be taken back to the former Campaign manager screen. Here, you will be able to develop additional ads, review, and submit your order. However, note that any campaign order you submit is reviewed by LinkedIn, so you may not see your ad immediately published.

To get the best outcome from your ads, you could try making a unique ad for every one of your buyer personas and alter the copy to go with it. That being said, below are a few LinkedIn ads copywriting tips:

Add a CTA (Call-to-Action)

When you add a CTA to your ad copy, which urges viewers to take action, it can help in enhancing the click rate of the add. For example:

- "Download this software now."

- "Click now to find out more."

This is a better approach, as opposed to writing an ad copy without any actionable steps.

Offer Value

You should clearly state the value for readers in your ad copy. Doing this can enhance the likelihood of people clicking on your ad. For instance, add something like "Offer valid while stocks last – Shop now," or "30% off for the first 5 buyers," you are sending an explicit message of what a person stands to benefit by clicking on your ad.

Testing

Test your ad copy. This should not scare you. You can develop numerous variants of your ad in every campaign. Doing this will let you experiment with various copy and images in the ads, to learn which is more suitable for your audience.

Analyzing your LinkedIn Ad Campaign

Now, you have finally kicked off your ad campaign, but you still are not done yet. There is still the vital aspect of any campaign, which is the analytics. LinkedIn ensures it is not difficult to monitor your campaign progress using the Campaign Manager dashboard. Here, you will be able to view the numerous chats which measure how your campaigns are performing. These measure areas like CTR, clicks, and expenditures. You will also be able to monitor your conversations by utilizing the graphs close to the end of the dashboard. Now that you know how to launch a campaign, you need to learn how to make it better, so you get the best performance from each ad.

Optimizing Your Ad Campaigns

It is always possible to enhance social ad campaigns. You need to know that the platform, content, and audience will always change. Below are a few methods of optimizing your ad campaign:

Optimizing Campaigns That Are Not Performing as They Should

If you have campaigns that are not performing as they are supposed to, there are some steps you can take to help them improve. They include:

Check the Click-through Rate of Every campaign

Is there a campaign doing better than the rest? If yes, it may be best to pause those that are not performing as well. By default, LinkedIn will show the campaigns that are less successful at a reduced rate, so it may be best to reduce the resources you invest in them. Rather, channeling more resources to ads that are performing exceptionally would have a higher possibility of achieving your marketing objectives.

Alter a Variable

If you have an ad which is not performing as it should, it does not mean you need to forgo the ad entirely. Experiment with diverse variations of one ad to note what is helping it succeed or stopping it from succeeding. Replace the image, edit the copy, update your bids, or alter the attributes of the target audience. But, ensure you do each of these one at a time, or you won't be able to tell which to correct.

Frequently Update your audience attributes

Refresh your knowledge of your target audience each month. Things tend to change so you may want to carry out new research on the attributes of your audience, which may have to be altered on your campaign. Ensure you frequently update these attributes, so your ads are always being viewed by the ideal audience.

Measuring Your Ad leads using Post-Click Reporting

The instant people have started to click on your ads, the next step is to find out if your ads are bringing in ideal traffic to your site. LinkedIn would be unable to tell you this, so you may have to carry out some reporting on these campaigns to find out more about the kind of traffic you are getting.

How can you determine this? You can do this using "gated" forms and offer. Anytime a person clicks on your ad and is directed to your site, gating content you are providing using a lead form will aid you in getting the information you require to determine if an individual is a significant lead or isn't. Link the form to any CRM software your organization is using, so the instant the information comes in, your sales team can make a move using it.

However, don't ignore your ad campaigns and pay attention to only the information you get from the form. Do the LinkedIn ads generate you qualified traffic? Is it generating users who convert to clients? If this is not the case, you may have to optimize your campaigns more.

For instance, if your LinkedIn ads are focused on individuals working in companies with 200-500 people, but you learn that most of the deals you close come from companies with 10-200 people, then you need to stop spending funds to target those larger organizations on LinkedIn.

The options for targeting we have covered in this chapter will let you alter any criteria of your choice, so ensure you capitalize on it. With the appropriate strategy and level of patience, LinkedIn ad campaigns can play a great role in ensuring your company achieves success in marketing and sales. Don't ignore LinkedIn when putting your social campaign list in place. An optimized and properly researched campaign can draw in tons of leads and sales to your company.

Chapter 9

Steps in Developing a Great LinkedIn Marketing Funnel

LinkedIn is a platform for professionals in business which is extremely valuable. With its members crossing more than 500million, it can be an excellent platform to get qualified leads which you can transform to sales.

However, the vital aspect is to understand how to draw in those prospects, and this is where your marketing funnel plays a huge role. Before we go any further, let us explore what a funnel means.

Funnels: What Are They?

When you direct a visitor to your site, your goal is to make them take specific actions. This could be to get them to sign up, buy a product, or fill a form. The moment a person carries out your intended action, it is called a conversion. The individual who visits your page converts from looking around, to taking your desired action.

Your funnel makes up the steps the visitor has to go through before they can successfully convert.

Stages of a Funnel

From the time your prospect comes across what you offer, until he/she purchases from you, they go through a range of stages in your funnel. The route taken by prospects may differ based on your niche, buying personas, and the sort of products or services you offer.

Before creating your marketing funnel, you need a clear vision for your business. You also have to put a marketing strategy in place and then define your target audience. All of these will ensure you work towards the goal of your business. A funnel can consist of as many stages as you deem suitable; however, generally, these are the core stages you need to note:

- Awareness: When the prospect finds out about your product, service, or solution.

- Decision: Here, the prospect is trying to choose if he/she wants the solution or product you have on offer.

- Action: Here, the prospect is transforming into an actual buyer by completing the transaction with you.

- Retention: This is the final stage, where you keep your client onboard your organization.

Having covered the stages in a funnel, let's move on to how you can create a successful marketing funnel for your company on LinkedIn.

Step 1: Locate Your Prospects and Connect

Locating your prospects and connecting with them on LinkedIn is a vital part of the process. You need to learn as much as you possibly can about your ideal clients.

To start, provide answers to the following questions:

- Who are your ideal clients? Are they on LinkedIn?

- What is the primary language of their industry, business, or company?

- What types of issues do they deal with?

Next, you need to ponder on the titles of those who take decisions. These should be the person you are in search of. For instance: VP of Marketing, Chief Marketer, etc.

If you want to take it a bit further, you can learn the industries they work in, and where they are situated. This could be based on a country or city. The instant you have gathered all of this data, you can locate your prospects using the Advanced search offered by LinkedIn.

LinkedIn Advanced Search

This is a great tool to use in locating prospects. The LinkedIn Advanced Search offers to screen data using precise factors to locate your target market.

For instance, let's say your perfect clients are VPs of Marketing. All you need to do is input VP Marketing in the search bar, then select the 'People' option. Next, make your result better by not selecting your 1st-degree connections, so the result does not show those you are already connected with.

To streamline it even further and get better results, you can use the Advanced search filters offered by LinkedIn like current organizations, location, and a host of other applicable options. If the results of the search are excellent, you may need to save them. To do this, select the option, 'Create a search alert' in the 'Saved Searches' box. You can find this in the right part of the search results.

This is a very beneficial tool because you will be provided search alerts straight from LinkedIn when there are new members on the platform that fit those criteria. You can head back to view these results any time you want to look for new prospects and leads. Then, you can check-out every profile to contact anyone who aligns with your criteria of an ideal customer.

Send a Personalized Request to Connect

The instant you have found a few prospects, send a connection request. When you do, as we have covered in earlier chapters, make sure the connection request is personalized to the individual you are sending to.

When you request to connect, the person you want to connect with is sent a default request, and many of them start to wonder about your reason for wanting to connect with them. By personalizing your request, you are immediately answering that question even before they ask, and this will urge your prospect in connecting. When putting together your message to connect, ensure you set it up from the perspective of the prospect instead of yours.

Another major risk you expose yourself to if you don't personalize your request is that when your prospect decides to hit the ignore button, they are also given the option of clicking the *I don't know this person* button. If you rack up a lot of these, you will find yourself dealing with an account restriction from LinkedIn.

Step 2: Engage and Develop a Relationship

When a person has accepted your request to connect, put together a process you will utilize in developing a relationship with him/her in person. To begin, you would want to know the person better and ensure you leave behind a positive impression.

Do you just head up to them, say hi and tell them you have something to sell? Well, even if you choose to do so, your chances of landing the sale will be slim.

The first thing you need to do when your connection request has been accepted by your prospect is to thank them. In addition to this, you can show you are interested in them by asking a relevant question when beginning a conversation with them.

Lots of marketers make the mistake of amassing connections and never starting up a conversation with them. Then they later begin to wonder why they have been unable to convert anyone. This is similar to heading to an event for networking, collecting lots of business cards, and dumping them on your office table without making a move. This is equivalent to you not attending the event at all.

Step 3: Offer Value & Develop Trust

The relationship building process goes beyond sending a follow-up message. To keep the conversation going, you need to send more messages that add value to the individual you just connected with, along with their business as often as you can.

Here, you have to develop trust with your new connection. You do this by offering them value by posting educational, insightful, and entertaining information that will assist them in their business or job. You can also send them valuable information through private messages.

You don't have to be the one who created the content; any publisher would do. However, you need to ensure that any content you choose to go with has to do with assisting your connection in dealing with a problem or challenge they are dealing with.

Once more, remember that this is not the time to give your prospect a sales pitch. Your objective is to nurture the relationship and enhance the level of trust. You can also achieve this by placing yourself as a resource or an individual who offers value and is a leader in his field.

When trying to determine the content you want to share, the following are a few questions to consider:

- What do they have an interest in?

- What is vital to them?

- What issues do they deal with?

Step 4: Develop Relationships

There are a range of ways you can nurture relationships. For one, you can show interest in a person, teaching them something, assisting them in any form, and interacting with them to know them better.

So how do you develop relationships with individuals you just connected with? Below are some ideas:

- Take note of what they post, leave comments and like them

- Link them up with another person in your network who would be of benefit to them

- Share relevant content of high quality with them, which has to do with the present issues they are dealing with or the problems that have to do with their field

- Ask appropriate questions so you can get to know them more

- Take note of trigger events which you can use to begin conversations regularly

- Follow them on other social channels and interact with them there too

Don't forget that most people won't be bothered so much about you until they see how caring you are. Your objective here is to remain in their minds, develop trust, and offer value.

Step 5: Take the Conversation Offline

The last step in the marketing funnel is to take the conversion to an offline location. The reason is, most of the time, if you want to convert someone to a client, you need to have an offline conversation. This is not applicable all the time, but it still is useful.

For instance, you will need to reach out to a person interested in your home decoration services in person. However, if someone has an interest in a course you offer online, then the conversation does not have to go online.

In essence, in the world of marketing and sales, you will not be able to develop a relationship with a prospect without taking the conversation offline at some point. The instant rapport has been established, and you have developed some trust and provided your prospect with value, so you will not be overstepping it if you ask for an offline conversation. A good amount of your prospects won't mind having an offline conversation with you regardless of if it is in-person meetings, video, or phone calls.

You get to know more about your prospect, understand the issues they are facing, and at the right time, provide your solution offline, where you convert prospects to clients. Remember that you can include as many steps as you want in your marketing funnel. You do not have to follow these steps rigidly. Only you know what works for you and your business.

Right now, there is no other online platform that has successfully gathered all the professionals in the globe in one location, with a business mindset while engaging with others there. This is the truth about LinkedIn, and that is the reason why, if you know how to digitally look for the right prospects and convert them using the appropriate funnel, as we have covered above, it can be a consistent source of new clients and qualified leads.

Chapter 10

Essential Tools and Apps to Utilize

To guarantee your success in the future as an entrepreneur, a business owner, and an individual in the marketing sector, it is vital that you take advantage of some of the most efficient LinkedIn marketing tools to better your business strategy. LinkedIn was designed to provide entrepreneurs, marketers, and people who own businesses a platform for building a good working relationship, collaborating, and connecting in ways that can help them get to the next level of success in business and be of help in getting others to the top. LinkedIn offers businesses lots of advantages, but if you are a newbie on LinkedIn or not very sure of how to navigate through this social media platform when putting up a profile on LinkedIn, you might not have the confidence to get into the LinkedIn marketing sector.

You have to take advantage of the very best of LinkedIn marketing tools if you must get your LinkedIn strategy to another level. In this chapter, we will be looking at apps and tools that can make your use of LinkedIn a little more effortless and very efficient and can go a long way in helping you see the world from a bigger perspective and achieve your desired result. Let's set the ball rolling.

LinkedIn Sales Navigator

Do you have the desire to boost sales with the use of LinkedIn? You can get started with sales navigator tool. This tool aims to build a bridge between buyers and sellers in a peculiar way, and it is made available by the social media marketing platform.

127

LinkedIn Sales Navigator comes with a lot of features. The most vital of these features include;

- Tools for building relationships which help you to get closer to your aim of achieving a sale gradually.

- Sales insight which has sales navigator as its source and ensures you can access the best data as one saddled with the responsibility of making decisions.

- It locates prospects that are most suitable for the things you have to offer by making use of a better-developed algorithm.

As you gain access to lead recommendations, it becomes possible to build a connection with, as well as sell to every prospect with the use of the many tools associated with Sales Navigator.

Sales Navigator is not guaranteed to move your revenue and sales to heights you have never experienced. It, however, can help you get started. Very frequently, new features are added by LinkedIn to sales navigator. This leads to a variety of more features while you make use of it.

Webfluential

There are various ways in which a marketing strategy can be generated. Of these ways, one of the most famous involves the use of influencers. If you must connect with the best influencers, one LinkedIn marketing tool to make use of is Webfluential. Webfluential connects top influencers in a field with enterprises that require help to develop a more effective brand outreach. It does this by working with large, as well as small businesses. Give Webfluential room to locate your perfect match and allow them to help your brand grow.

LinkedIn Plugins

If you are looking to making LinkedIn functionality a part of your website, LinkedIn plugins can come in very handy.

A lot of individuals do not consider this a direct method of impacting social selling, as well as sales. They are, however, letting a major privilege pass them by. Below are some plugins you can take advantage of;

- Company Profile

- Follow Company

- Share

- Alumni Tool

- Member Profile

- LinkedIn AutoFill

- Company Insider

- Job and Job Titles You Have an Interest In.

An example is you might want to share the profile of your company with individuals that visit your website. Doing this helps them have a vivid idea of what exactly your organization stands for. It also helps them know about those that you are affiliated with.

LinkedIn plugins can help increase sales but are not the most efficient strategy for those looking to increase sales. They, however, can help your audience have more facts about your business, thereby making them get in touch with you.

eLink Pro

eLink Pro is a tool that works with the ideology that if you check out other people's profile on LinkedIn, they will also check out yours. Although this sounds true, it has a challenge. This challenge is visiting lots of profiles can be very tasking. This even becomes more pronounced if the only profiles that you have any interest in are those that you consider qualified prospects.

When making use of eLink Pro, you can automate this process. It can pay a visit to up to 800 profiles in 24 hours. Although this does not guarantee that these people visited will, in turn, visit your profile, there is a massive likelihood that up to 10% of these profiles visited will visit your profile. The implication of this is you will have about 40 people checking out your profile daily. Out of these forty people, some of them might end up qualifying as leads.

This concept is a simple one, and it works. All you need to do is attract as much interest as you can on LinkedIn, and the way to go about this is by visiting a vast number of profiles.

Crystal

There are times when a social media marketing tool, which is a lot different from other tools around it, pops up. This is one thing you get when you take advantage of Crystal, also called the "world's largest personality platform." Crystal can have a review of a premium account or LinkedIn profile and go on to make insight, as well as a feedback into the personality of the person involved.

When you have information like this at your fingertips, carrying out a conversation in a manner that is considered appropriate will become easy. You do not have to make a call and sound all cold because you know nothing about the person at the other end.

130

Comparing a couple of LinkedIn profiles might only make you notice the same thing. However, by making use of Crystal, you can easily discover the many areas available to be taken advantage of and used to avoid the much disliked cold call.

Becoming a better coordinator is vital for anyone that is looking to better their LinkedIn social selling. With access to this tool, you will not have to put in a lot of effort before you can make an important alteration and replace a cold shoulder with a lead builder prospect.

LeadGrabber Pro

One very vital step in marketing is putting up leads of good quality which guarantee future sales and future customers. While generating leads is possible, it does not come so easy. As a result of this, software such as Lead Grabber Pro can be of help. LeadGrabber Pro is considered one of the best tools for LinkedIn marketing. It puts together a list of likely clients from highly rated networking sites like LinkedIn. This can help you discover the most trusted leads for your enterprise. LeadGrabber Pro can go through social media platforms, as well as the capacity to generate an email list that can be used for outreach and newsletter. This explains why B2B marketers make use of it.

Dux-Soup

If your business must move from one level to another, you will have to generate fresh leads. With Dux-Soup, you can put your attention on the need to build these relationships and at the same time take part in the heavy lifting that is associated with getting their interest. Dux-Soup was designed basically for LinkedIn, and it can be used to build your brand, develop fresh business leads, develop your profile of sales campaign that is targeted, thereby ensuring that you are in charge of happenings. Dux-Soup is a LinkedIn tool everyone should have as it can go a long way in helping you have free time to put your attention on growth and expansion.

LinkedIn Small Business

By making use of this tool alongside its three-stage approach to being a fantastic lead builder and social seller, your business will be positioned appropriately to develop trust, have increased sales, and accomplish quite a number of associated goals. These guide which can be broken down to three stages are:

- Build a connection with your audience

- Inaugurate the presence of your brand

- Get them engaged with the use of content marketing

From this approach, step three is very vital to marketers. The reason for this is, it allows you to create, as well as share content marketing skills, which are of good value with your chosen audience. When you do this, you can get the attention of prospects. That, however, is not all. You can offer them the much-needed encouragement to be in charge of making decisions.

When on LinkedIn Small Business Center, there is a lot you can learn. This implies that you take out time to go through absolutely all the features that you come across carefully. By doing this, you no doubt will be able to come across a strategy that will be ideally suited for your sales targets.

LeadFuze

LinkedIn comes with lots of benefits. Of all these benefits, one is a primary challenge that a lot of sales professionals have to deal with. What could this challenge be? This challenge is the presence of over 610 million members.

If you lack a tool to help with processing, in no time, you will be overwhelmed by the available data and might not know how to help yourself. This is the exact reason for the popularity of LeadFuze. With LeadFuze, it is easy to rapidly develop a list of target accounts, as well as leads by carrying out some search.

The lead collection procedure is something to take seriously. There is, however, more to it. You will have to diligently remain a lead builder. Individuals that make use of this tool are also able to access contact information such as phone numbers and email, therefore, making the process involved in sales an easy one to begin.

There is more. With LeadFuze, it is easy to automatically send follow-ups and emails. At the moment, you can get details about over 200 million premium accounts and B2B professionals. Also, as customers put up about 350,000 prospects every month, you will have no issues having a collection of leads.

LeadFuze is regarded as one of the best complete LinkedIn tools for lead generation. It can automatically expose some of the most vital details, therefore playing a major role in boosting your media marketing strategy.

Outro

Outro can help you uncover prospective clients from more than one source. The sources you can discover potential clients from are;

- The Outro community

- Your Network

As you already know, you can go through LinkedIn for hours in search of premium accounts only for you to come to the discovery that there are no qualified prospects within your reach.

With Outro, you can avoid wasting time and carry out your search more efficiently. This is possible because of its distinctive "relationship strength algorithm." As soon as you make any request, the other duties are done by the tool.

Other features are:

- The alternative to developing reports

- The capacity to get contact data exported

- Incorporation with virtually all CRM.

If you don't want to go through LinkedIn in search of premium accounts, as well as qualified leads, then you should try Outro. Outro features an exceptional and efficient algorithm, which makes it easy to get your network expanded and locate prospects that are qualified.

Salestools.io

Salestools.io is a software for lead generation, which makes use of a different approach. It allows its users to download lead lists to excel from LinkedIn. If you prefer tracking leads this way, this might just be the perfect tool for you.

Not all tools come with the ability to get data downloaded to excel. So, if you come across a tool that can do this, it is enormous. There is, however, more to this tool.

As soon as you get a list of your prospects, you can go to the next stage of sending every one of them an email. Salestool.io can be of help to you while you get this done.

Salestool has a feature which makes it easy to get outreach messages personalized. This feature is known as sequences. It also helps you keep track of your activities in a bid to drive leads through the use of your sales funnel in any way that pleases you.

This tool cannot be considered one of the most developed on this list. However, if you are looking for ways to skyrocket your sales on LinkedIn, it is an excellent tool.

Discoverly

Although LinkedIn is considered a top-notch professional networking service, it does not stop you from finding out the activities of your connections on other social media platforms other than LinkedIn.

Discoverly can come in handy if you want to do this. When you pay an individual's LinkedIn profile a visit, all the information you will be able to access are those from LinkedIn. But this can change if you make use of Discoverly. With Discoverly, you can have access to other details as far as social media is concerned. An example of this is letting you know if you have mutual friends on Facebook. This can help make the connection even more profound.

Sales is basically about building a connection with prospects that are qualified. With Discoverly, you can have lots of different information in a place.

Note: To make use of Discoverly, you need to access the internet with Chrome browser.

Rapportive

Do you make use of Gmail? If yes, you can convert your inbox into an efficient tool for LinkedIn sales. You can achieve this by taking advantage of Rapportive. As soon as you get the free add-on for Firefox or Chrome installed, LinkedIn profile information is brought to Gmail by Rapportive.

So, there will be no need for moving between various tabs. You can get all you need to get about your contacts from your inbox.

A perfect example is this; you get an email from an individual that is interested in carrying out a transaction with you. When this happens, Rappotive can make the following available to you:

- Location

- Shared connection

- LinkedIn profile. This includes company title and name.

LinkedIn Elevate

There are lots of essential aspects of making use of social media to boost your reach and make your message noticed. Of all these aspects, the content that you create, as well as that which you curate is one of the most important. With LinkedIn Elevate, the sharing of content has become very easy. This, therefore, makes it one of the best marketing tools on LinkedIn. Elevate is both a mobile app and a desktop application. Also, it makes use of its algorithm to scan their news sources. This helps it suggest articles which you should share on your LinkedIn profile. You can have a lot of time for doing other profitable things if you have a means of discovering relatable content which you can put up.

<u>Guru</u>

If you are working as a single individual or you are a part of or leading a sales marketing team, you definitely will want to function in the fastest and smartest way possible. Guru can help you with this.

To make use of LinkedIn in boosting sales as an individual in charge of making decisions implies that you will have to spend a lot of time going through the profiles, as well as pages of various companies. This seems serious but is just the beginning. What is important is what you make out of the information that you come across.

By taking into account a lot of information from every prospect, Guru can make certain things available. These are:

- Active customers that are currently working in the industry you work in

- Potential competitors

- Sales have a lot to do with the industry of the prospect.

Guru can help you discover a lot of prospects in a very brief period. It is not a break from the norm to put your attention on just one lead and rely on Guru to make available other leads with the same space. Finally, Guru makes many tools that teams can make use of in sharing information available.

SalesLoft

There are lots of essential aspects of owning a business. However, one of the most vital is making, as well as closing sales regularly. This can be done with the use of SalesLoft. To a large extent, SalesLoft has come very close to perfecting the process of sales engagement and is therefore efficient at building a bridge between consumer and business owner very quickly. This makes it one of the most efficient LinkedIn marketing tools that every business person should make use of. SalesLoft helps in building real connections, getting you sales strategy personal, making data-driven results available which can help direct your sales technique, making it an excellent investment which can always come in handy when it is needed.

Voogy

This was formerly known as Salestool.io. It is a marketing automation tool that is intent-driven and can bring about an improvement to your business strategy, as well as your inbound and outbound lead engagement. As far as LinkedIn marketing tools are concerned, we want to ensure we do all that is in our power to ensure that the leads we intend to generate are nurtured. But things can appear funny if we do not have time on our hands for all we need to do. At this point, we will need marketing automation to help with our marketing strategy.

LinkedIn Marketing Tools: Ensuring You Are Making Use of the Best

There are lots of people on LinkedIn. This makes it expedient that you have the very best LinkedIn marketing tools in your armory. These great tools can cover lead generation, ensure that your audience follows the content you create and help you develop a LinkedIn marketing strategy that will bring about good results. Each one of these tools offers something unique that can go a long way in making your business plans more efficient, a lot easier to make use of, and also make sure you have some of the most trusted LinkedIn marketing tools for the growth of your business.

Using Tools the Right Way

If you use them appropriately, LinkedIn tools can be trusted to deliver excellent lead generation without you having to suffer from any bans or restrictions on the LinkedIn platform.

What exactly is safe usage? It is recommended that you calculate your LinkedIn Range (LR). Your LinkedIn Range is 3.5-55% of all your connections.

For instance, 5,000 contacts will place your LinkedIn Range at around 150-250. If you are using LinkedIn Sales Navigator, you need to note that you have a limit of 500 profile views each day. You need to see this as the max you can do. Practically, most users will have fewer connections on the platform, which means their LR won't be as high.

LinkedIn Tools can Establish Compound Connection Growth

Get started by selecting a figure that aligns with your LinkedIn Range. So, if you have 2,000 connections, your LinkedIn automation tool should be set with the LinkedIn Range upper limit of a hundred new connection requests in a single day.

You can set your LinkedIn tool to only visit 100 profiles daily, without the need to send any requests to connect. Naturally, a number of these contacts will go through your profile as a way of returning the favor. With a well optimized LinkedIn profile, you will get several connection requests.

Also, you have to be active on LinkedIn. Like we have covered in the earlier chapters, You can do this by sharing posts, liking posts, and putting up original content. These activities are regarded as interactions, and they can bring about an inflow of connection requests

However, it is essential to establish limits while working with LinkedIn. Your business goals might tempt you to go beyond such limits. It, however, is vital to be cautious and stay within whatever limits you set.

Permanent Restrictions Are Rare, but You Risk Facing One

The fear of being banned or facing a permanent LinkedIn account restriction has made a lot of people that make use of LinkedIn tools to reduce their level of activity. At some point, there were reports that an update to the platform was targeting a specific automation tool which scared a lot of users.

The truth is LinkedIn is continuously changing. It does this to innovate its algorithm. This is one reason it is very successful.

On the flip side of the coin are some companies that make automation solutions available for LinkedIn. These companies are always in a race and try to look for a solution each time LinkedIn goes through an update.

These companies are usually successful in getting an update. This explains why the three most successful tools for LinkedIn automation in the Chrome Web Store share more than 100,000 downloads.

Good Housekeeping Practices for LinkedIn Tools

As far as automation is involved, good housekeeping practices are important. This can be likened to making use of the right housing practices in tidying up your home. A very crucial practice you need to carry out frequently is to get rid of any pending sent connection requests.

If you have lots of outstanding connection requests, LinkedIn can see it as a red flag and might interpret it as an attempt to get in touch with people that don't know you. Frequently getting rid of old connection requests which were not accepted, will help you stay safe. Typically, if you are more targeted in the LinkedIn growth strategy, you will have less outstanding requests.

Effective Tools Behave Like the Real User

Search for an automated tool which you can configure to act the way you act on LinkedIn. One way to stay safe while using LinkedIn is to set limits for yourself based on your LR.

To be in charge of smart automation, search for features like go/pause/ stop. This will help you put up limits and make whatever automation tool you are working with, act as you would act.

Think about this; if the automation tool you are making use of is so busy by 3.am, it will be very easy to suspect you for making use of third-party tools.

Not All Tools Offer the Same Functionalities

There is a range of tools which include software programs, browser extensions, and plug-ins, third-party tools, and bots. However, you need to obtain the appropriate tools to get the job done.

Not every tool comes with the same quality. Do your research to determine if the team responsible for the tool has a consistent track record. Ask yourself the following:

- How do they provide support?

- Are they accessible?

- Is it possible to speak to the individuals responsible for the tool?

It's not a strange occurrence for a LinkedIn tool to suddenly vanish. How old a tool is may not be a great way to determine if it will exist later in the future, but it may be a safer option to go with more established and older tools.

Watch out for genuine testimonials that demonstrate actual ROI. You can't get any evidence more effective than seeing the way organizations in an industry similar to yours use LinkedIn tools to meet needs similar to yours.

Be a Resource

It is not adequate to grow an elaborate network on LinkedIn. You have to take it further if you desire to make conversions from your network. A great way to begin is to provide a new prospect something of value. This could be content you believe they may have an interest in or a blog post you wrote.

Most users who have successfully used a tool on LinkedIn, have first considered the value he/she can provide, which is what is essential before using a tool. Put a value you can offer in place and let your tool help you achieve this value.

That being said, let's take a look at some of the best practices to consider when using a tool.

- Be careful when using tools

- Consider your goals, the individual you want to reach, and what will urge them to respond to a request to connect?

- Always follow the LinkedIn fair usage limit, or you may have to deal with penalties.

- Try to be as targeted as possible. The rewards are enormous

142

- For a better response rate, ensure your interactions are personalized

- Plan for how to use the additional time you get: where can you productively divert that in your organization?

Getting around LinkedIn Usage Limits

There are LinkedIn connection tools that come with helpful workarounds. These well-designed workarounds make it possible to make use of LinkedIn without having to think about any connection limits. One of these tools makes use of Google in tapping into search results obtained from LinkedIn.

The amazing thing about making use of this approach is your LinkedIn Connection limits for the month is not affected. This may be a great choice if you don't want to purchase a premium subscription.

When Not to Use Tools On LinkedIn

Having understood why tools can be of benefit to you on LinkedIn, you need to also understand that there are instances where using tools may not be a great idea.

It is dependent on the audience you are targeting. For instance, a CEO of one of the top companies in their sector would be unlikely to approve a connection from an individual they have not met before or done business with. However, they may accept a connection request from another CEO.

Using tools for automation on LinkedIn may offer you lots of benefits, but sending out numerous connection requests may not be the way to go.

Conclusion

Congratulations!! You made it to the end of this fascinating journey. This goes to show how serious you are about understanding the nitty-gritty of what LinkedIn has to offer you. If you have not started thinking of ways you can incorporate LinkedIn in your marketing strategy, I am sure you already understand the kind of opportunities you are letting slip by.

LinkedIn has proven that even though it does not have the same amount of users you will find on other social media platforms, it remains an excellent platform for generating leads and converting these leads into buyers. Remember the steps we have covered in this book. To begin, create an appealing profile which is buyer-focused and not about you. If you want to clinch that sale, you have to keep your buyer in mind. Next, show build rapport and trust by staying consistent. Share actionable, high-quality content that is relevant to your audience as frequently as you can. Do not rack up those connections only to vanish from the platform for days without posting any content. Lastly, take advantage of LinkedIn ads to further your reach.

All of these tips and many more have been covered in this book, and will surely help you grow. All you need to do is follow these steps, and you will become an authority your audience comes to when they need a service or product similar to offer.

Remember, like all other social media strategies, growing your connection requires dedication and patience. Do not expect to get all the leads you want overnight, or jump from 0 -5,000 connections. Nonetheless, if you can implement the strategies you learn here the right way, the possibilities would be limitless.

Bibliographies

LinkedIn Claims Half a Billion Users. (2019). Retrieved from http://fortune.com/2017/04/24/linkedin-users/

Cooper, P. (2019). 16 LinkedIn Statistics That Matter to Marketers in 2019. Retrieved from https://blog.hootsuite.com/linkedin-statistics-business/

Yurieff, K. (2019). Facebook hits 2 billion monthly users. Retrieved from https://money.cnn.com/2017/06/27/technology/facebook-2-billion-users/index.html

The Global Trends That Will Shape Recruiting In 2015 [INFOGRAPHIC]. (2014). Retrieved from http://talent.linkedin.com/blog/index.php/2014/11/the-global-trends-that-will-shape-recruiting-in-2015

Tiwari, S. (2019). Importance of LinkedIn Marketing - Parangat's Blog. Retrieved from https://www.parangat.com/blog/importance-of-linkedin-marketing/

[INFOGRAPHIC] Q2 2013: The State of LinkedIn. (2019). Retrieved from http://blog.wishpond.com/post/54116170504/infographic-q2-2013-the-state-of-linkedin

The Sophisticated Guide to Marketing on LinkedIn. (2019). Retrieved from https://business.linkedin.com/marketing-solutions/c/14/1/sophisticated-guide-for-marketing

DeMers, J. 10 Reasons Your Brand Needs To Be On LinkedIn. Retrieved from https://www.forbes.com/sites/jaysondemers/2015/07/22/10-

reasons-your-brand-needs-to-be-on-linkedin/#67bb48a23aca

Tiwari, S. (2019). Importance of LinkedIn Marketing - Parangat's Blog. Retrieved from https://www.parangat.com/blog/importance-of-linkedin-marketing/

Osman, M. (2019). Mind-Blowing LinkedIn Statistics and Facts (2019). Retrieved from https://kinsta.com/blog/linkedin-statistics/

The Deep Disconnect: An HR Data Report. Retrieved from https://getbambu.com/data-reports/deep-disconnect-hr-report/

14 LinkedIn Hacks That Will Triple the Size of Your Network in Two Weeks. (2017). Retrieved from https://blog.crazyegg.com/2016/08/29/14-linkedin-hacks-triple-network/

York, A. (2019). 5 LinkedIn Best Practices for Marketing Professionals. Retrieved from https://sproutsocial.com/insights/linkedin-best-practices/

Walters, L. (2015). 10 statistics that show video is the future of marketing | MWP Digital Media. Retrieved from https://mwpdigitalmedia.com/blog/10-statistics-that-show-video-is-the-future-of-marketing/

Lloyd, D. (2015). SEO for Success in Video Marketing | Adobe Blog. Retrieved from https://theblog.adobe.com/seo-for-success-in-video-marketing/

Nguyen, C. (2015). 12 Webinar Stats You Need to Know. Retrieved from https://www.readytalk.com/blog/christine-nguyen/12-webinar-stats-you-need-to-know

Gibbs, A. (2019). How to Start a Podcast for Your Company. Retrieved from https://blog.spinweb.net/facts-about-business-podcasting-that-will-blow-your-mind

www.ingramcontent.com/pod-product-compliance
Lightning Source LLC
LaVergne TN
LVHW022321060326
832902LV00020B/3593